PARENTING

with

SCRIPTURE

PARENTING with SCRIPTURE

A TOPICAL GUIDE FOR TEACHABLE MOMENTS

KARA DURBIN

MOODY PRESS
CHICAGO

Library of Congress Cataloging-in-Publication Data

Durbin, Kara
    Parenting with Scripture: a topical guide for teachable moments/Kara
      Durbin. p.cm.
    Includes index.
    ISBN 0-8024-6542-0
    1. Christian education of children. 2. Christian education—Home
training. 3. Christian ethics—Biblical teaching. 4. Children—Religious
life. I. Title.

BV1590 .D87 2001
248.8'45—dc21
                           00-046925

7 9 10 8 6

Printed in the United States of America

Dedicated to
my mother,
who blessed my life
by parenting me with Scripture

*All Scripture is God-breathed and is useful for teaching,
rebuking, correcting and training in righteousness,
so that the man of God may be
thoroughly equipped for every good work.*
2 Timothy 3:16–17

CONTENTS

INTRODUCTION

WAYS TO USE THIS BOOK

This book is a . . .

Reference for "teachable moments":

- ○ This book can serve as a launch pad for discussing topics related to situations your child tells you about or is dealing with, news reports, TV show scenarios . . .

Communication facilitator:

- ○ When a child asks, or when you wonder, "What does God say about . . ."
- ○ When a child asks, "What does ___ mean?"
- ○ As an opening to help you find out what your child knows and does not know about each topic.

Topical devotional guide for your child or family.

Scripture reference for memory work:

- ○ It gives you and your child verses you can memorize that pertain to the situations you deal with most often.

Prayer guide:

- ○ Pick a verse a day and pray those words for yourself and your child.
- ○ Ask God to help you know how to best communicate and teach each topic to your child.
- ○ Ask God to help you set a good example in each area.

FEATURES AND SYMBOLS
Italicized Scripture
Portions of Scripture in each topic are italicized to help parents of younger children quickly pull out the most concise and easily understood parts.

Key Symbols
Small icons appear beside many Scripture passages and Scripture verse references in this book. These symbols are given to help you recognize that a Scripture is pulled from a one of several familiar and especially important Bible passages. The Scripture Appendix at the end of the book gives the complete passage.

📖 The Ten Commandments

☺ The Beatitudes

♥ The Love Chapter

🍇 The Fruit of the Spirit

🛡 The Armor of God

🪝 Clothe Yourself with . . .

➕ Add to Your Faith . . .

HELPFUL TIPS

Parenting with Scripture can be used for twos through teens. The verses and discussions can be geared toward what your child can understand, and the Take Action activities can be adapted to the child's age, interest, and ability. It is never too early or too late to begin instilling these principles in your child. Do not neglect your job as a teacher of these subjects.

These commandments that I give you today are to be upon your hearts. Impress them on your children. Talk about them when you sit at home and when you walk along the road, when you lie down and when you get up. (Deuteronomy 6:6–7)

Train a child in the way he should go, and when he is old he will not turn from it. (Proverbs 22:6)

The exciting part about using this book is that you are teaching your child to think through the Scripture and apply it to his life. This process will give the Bible meaning and make the words real to him. Most importantly, you will instill in your child a habit of turning to the Scripture to answer questions so that it will serve as the guidebook for life.

The discussion questions in this book will make you and your child think. Unfortunately, thinking is not encouraged enough in today's society. However, if you want your child to base his life and decision making on a firm biblical foundation, you must prepare him by helping him think through each of these topics. For example, when a question refers to a Scripture, give the child a chance to think and answer before reading the Scripture. Then discuss and compare his answer with God's Word. Through these discussions, you will learn what your child knows about the topic, what he is struggling with, what he does not understand, and what needs to be reinforced.

The verses given are by no means an exhaustive list. The concordance and index to subjects found in the back of most Bibles are good resources for finding more verses on each topic. If you happen upon helpful verses that are not listed in the book, write them in for future reference.

Help your child look up the verses in his Bible instead of always reading them from this book. Remember, this is just a reference book. You want to do all you can to reinforce the Bible with your child. Working with your child to look up the verses helps him become more familiar and comfortable with the Bible. When your child is old enough, let him underline the verses in the Bible and write the topics beside them. As he runs across them when using his Bible, these notes will serve as a reminder that he is already familiar with those verses. Allowing your child to mark verses in his Bible gives him a sense of ownership and understanding of the Bible and the joy that comes with stumbling upon familiar passages.

May your child learn to love the Lord with all his heart, soul, and strength (Deuteronomy 6:5).

WHY I WROTE THIS BOOK

A while back, my sister and I talked about a time when she caught her five-year-old son lying. She told him that he should always be honest, not only because she said so, but more importantly, because God said so. She then quoted a related Scripture to him and explained what it meant in reference to what he had done. I was amazed that she had the perfect verse ready to use in that teachable moment. I began to think through the different issues parents face with their children and questioned whether I knew verses for all the possible situations. This led me to an unsuccessful search for a topical Scripture reference for parents. Thus, in response to my own need and a desire to minister to other families, I began researching and writing. This book is a result of that study.

And this is my prayer: that your love may abound more and more in knowledge and depth of insight, so that you may be able to discern what is best and may be pure and blameless until the day of Christ, filled with the fruit of righteousness that comes through Jesus Christ—to the glory and praise of God.

Philippians 1:9–11

ACKNOWLEDGMENTS

Praise be to God for this wonderful surprise project He had in store for me.

Mom and Dad—God overwhelmingly blessed me with you as my parents! Saying thank you does not do justice for your providing me with a secure, Christian home and consistent love, support, and encouragement! I love you!

Tim—Thank you for your tireless and loving effort in helping me through every stage of this book. Your patience in dealing with my computer problems helped me keep my sanity.

Will and Susan—The Lord used you to inspire the book!

Katie Beth, Abby, Will, and Caroline—You are precious to me! Thank you for serving as the basis for the majority of the ideas in the book.

I am tremendously grateful to all my family, friends, and fellow Bible Study Fellowship members who diligently prayed me through this process. There were days that I was able to keep writing only because I knew you were praying. This book is a result of those fervent prayers.

A world of thanks to those who spent hours reading my manuscripts and giving me feedback. Those special people are Tim Durbin, Katharine Gentsch, Susan Gharis, Kay Gentsch, Michelle McNeill, and my editor, Anne Scherich.

To the gracious and friendly staff at Moody Press, who helped the book through its many stages, I am grateful.

ANGER

 **anger - n.** The strong feeling of being very annoyed.

Genesis 4:6–7
Then the LORD said to Cain, "Why are you angry? Why is your face downcast? If you do what is right, will you not be accepted? But if you do not do what is right, sin is crouching at your door; it desires to have you, but you must master it."

Psalm 37:8a
Refrain from anger and turn from wrath.

Proverbs 15:1
A gentle answer turns away wrath, but a harsh word stirs up anger.

Proverbs 22:24–25
Do not make friends with a hot-tempered man, do not associate with one easily angered, or you may learn his ways and get yourself ensnared.

Ephesians 4:26–27
"In your anger do not sin": Do not let the sun go down while you are still angry, and do not give the devil a foothold.

James 1:19–20
My dear brothers, take note of this: Everyone should be quick to listen, slow to speak and slow to become angry, for man's anger does not bring about the righteous life that God desires.

See also: Proverbs 14:17a, 29; 15:18; 29:22; Ecclesiastes 7:9; Ephesians 4:31.

Discussion:
Think of a recent time you were angry.

◆ Was it really worth getting angry?
◆ How could the situation have been handled differently?
◆ What does anger accomplish?

What are some methods that will help calm anger?
(See how many your child can think of on his own.)

> Take a deep breath and count to ten before reacting in anger. Use the time to think how you can calmly handle the situation. See Psalm 37:8a.

> Politely walk away and do not discuss the situation until you have had time to calm down. See Psalm 37:8a.

> Say a prayer over the situation, even if you only have a moment. Ask God to help you control your anger and deal with the situation in a reasonable manner. Read James 1:19–20.

> Remain calm and speak quietly when you feel the anger rising in you or the other person. Using this method in an intense situation will often speak more strongly then a loud, angry voice. See Proverbs 15:1.

Read and discuss the warnings about anger in Genesis 4:6–7 and Proverbs 22:24–25.

 **Take Action:**
1. Challenge each other (parent and child) to use one or more of the above methods for a week. After each situation, discuss how both of you fared with the tactics and what needs to be improved. Focusing on these strategies for a period of time will help them become habits.

2. Remember Ephesians 4:26 and try to work through any anger before bedtime.

APATHY

 **apathetic - adj.** If you are **apathetic,** you do not care about anything or want to do anything.

Genesis 25:34 (For context, read verses 29–34.)
Then Jacob gave Esau some bread and some lentil stew. He ate and drank, and then got up and left. So Esau despised his birthright.

John 10:11–13
"I am the good shepherd. The good shepherd lays down his life for the sheep. The hired hand is not the shepherd who owns the sheep. So when he sees the wolf coming, he abandons the sheep and runs away. Then the wolf attacks the flock and scatters it. The man runs away because he is a hired hand and cares nothing for the sheep."

Galatians 6:9
Let us not become weary in doing good, for at the proper time we will reap a harvest if we do not give up.

Colossians 3:23–24
Whatever you do, work at it with all your heart, as working for the Lord, not for men, since you know that you will receive an inheritance from the Lord as a reward. It is the Lord Christ you are serving.

Titus 3:14
Our people must learn to devote themselves to doing what is good, in order that they may provide for daily necessities and not live unproductive lives.

Hebrews 6:12
We do not want you to become lazy, but to imitate those who through faith and patience inherit what has been promised.

 **Discussion:**
Are you apathetic in any area of your life?

◆ What are the consequences of your apathy?

◆ Who does your apathy affect?

◆ Why should you work at not being apathetic?
Read Galatians 6:9.

Read what Jesus says in John 10:11–13 and discuss the apathy of the hired hand.

Sometimes apathy is simply caused by not thinking through your actions. Read about Esau's unfortunate moment of apathy and discuss the consequences. (Genesis 25:29–34; verse 34 listed).

Take Action:
Galatians 6:9 Chart:
Follow the example of the chart below and think through the consequences of your apathy in the areas with which you are struggling. Pray that you will "not become weary in doing good." After you have overcome the apathy, enjoy "reaping the harvest."

Area	Consequences of Apathy	Rewards of Not Being Apathetic
Homework	Low grades Discipline at home Might not pass Held back a grade Not be with friends	Good grades Not in trouble Stay on grade level Sense of achievement

APPRECIATION

appreciate - v. 1. To enjoy or value somebody or something. **2.** To understand something. *I appreciate your point of view.*

2 Kings 4:13

Elisha said to him, "*Tell her, 'You have gone to all this trouble for us. Now what can be done for you?* Can we speak on your behalf to the king or the commander of the army?'" She replied, "I have a home among my own people."

Psalm 100:4–5

Enter his gates with thanksgiving and his courts with praise; *give thanks to him and praise his name.* For the LORD is good and his love endures forever; his faithfulness continues through all generations.

Colossians 3:16

Let the word of Christ dwell in you richly as you teach and admonish one another with all wisdom, and as you sing psalms, hymns, and spiritual songs with gratitude in your hearts to God.

1 Thessalonians 5:12

Now we ask you, brothers, to respect those who work hard among you, who are over you in the Lord and who admonish you.

 **Discussion:**
How does appreciation go beyond thankfulness?[1]

◆ What are some things you appreciate? Why?

◆ Name some people you appreciate. Why?

◆ What are some things that have been done for you that you appreciate? Why?

 **Take Action:**
1. In 2 Kings 4:13, Elisha demonstrates a way to show your true appreciation when someone has done something special or thoughtful for you. Elisha says, "You have gone to all this trouble for us. Now what can be done for you?" Think of someone who has gone to some trouble for you. How can you express your appreciation? (Write a card, call or tell him in person, ask what you can do for him, make something for him . . .)

2. Follow the instructions in Colossians 3:16 and sing psalms, hymns, and spiritual songs to express your gratitude and appreciation to God. Invest in a hymnal, songbook, and/or tape, and memorize songs so that you can sing them anytime.

3. When writing thank-you notes, go beyond merely saying thank you. Try to genuinely express why you appreciate the gift, person, or action. For example, in Psalm 100:4–5, the writer not only instructs us to thank and praise God, but he also gives several reasons.

Parenting Tip:
Make thank-you notes mandatory. The child may see it as a chore, but it will instill in her a positive habit and cause him to take time to express appreciation.

Related topic: Thankfulness

---

1. Appreciation involves the understanding of the worth or importance of something.

ATTITUDE

attitude - n. Your opinions and feelings about someone or something. *Theo has a positive attitude toward his work.*

Ephesians 4:22–24

You were taught, with regard to your former way of life, to put off your old self, which is being corrupted by its deceitful desires; to be made new in the attitude of your minds; and to put on the new self, created to be like God in true righteousness and holiness.

Philippians 2:5

Your attitude should be the same as that of Christ Jesus.

Philippians 4:8

Finally, brothers, whatever is true, whatever is noble, whatever is right, whatever is pure, whatever is lovely, whatever is admirable—if anything is excellent or praiseworthy—think about such things.

Colossians 3:23–24

Whatever you do, work at it with all your heart, as working for the Lord, not for men, since you know that you will receive an inheritance from the Lord as a reward. It is the Lord Christ you are serving.

I Thessalonians 5:16–18

Be joyful always; pray continually; give thanks in all circumstances, for this is God's will for you in Christ Jesus.

See also: Ezra 6:22; Daniel 3:19

 **Discussion:**
Look up Ezra 6:22 and Daniel 3:19 and label each
verse as an example of a positive or negative attitude.

It is obvious from these two verses that your attitude affects
your actions. What else does your attitude affect?

* Others   * Your walk with God
* Your health   * Your words

Can your attitude work both for the positive as well as the
negative in each of the ways you just listed?

What do the Scriptures on the previous page say to you about
your attitude?

Take Action:
Parent: Soon after the next time your child has a bad
attitude, discuss the following.

1. Did your attitude help the situation?
2. Did your attitude hurt the situation?
3. How did your attitude affect the others around you?
   Ask them.
4. Do you think God was pleased with your attitude?
5. Consider how the situation could have been worse. Be
   thankful that wasn't the case.
6. How could you have handled the situation with a positive attitude?
7. What can you do as a reminder to have a better attitude in the future?
   o Memorize 1 Thessalonians 5:16–18.
   o Put a smiley face on your mirror so it is the first
     thing you see in the morning.

BEAUTY

 **beautiful - adj.** Very pleasant to look at or listen to.

I Samuel 16:7b
"Man looks at the outward appearance, but the LORD looks at the heart."

Psalm 27:4
One thing I ask of the LORD, this is what I seek: that I may dwell in the house of the LORD all the days of my life, to gaze upon the beauty of the LORD and to seek him in his temple.

Psalm 139:14
I praise you because I am fearfully and wonderfully made; your works are wonderful, I know that full well.

Proverbs 31:30
Charm is deceptive, and beauty is fleeting; but a woman who fears the LORD is to be praised.

I Peter 3:3–4
Your beauty should not come from outward adornment, such as braided hair and the wearing of gold jewelry and fine clothes. Instead, it should be that of your inner self, the unfading beauty of a gentle and quiet spirit, which is of great worth in God's sight.

Discussion:
Which is more important, a person's inner or outer beauty? Read 1 Samuel 16:7b.; Proverbs 31:30; and 1 Peter 3:3–4.

Discuss the following sayings:

- ◆ "Beauty is in the eye of the beholder."
  —Eighteenth-century proverb
- ◆ "Never judge a book by its cover."
  —*American Speech*, 1929

Take Action:
Draw a picture of yourself with only the outlines and write words on it that describe how you are internally beautiful. Title the picture, "Beautiful me!" Think of an internal area where you are not so beautiful. Cut out a strip of paper, write that word on it, and attach it to your hand on the picture. Give that area a "make-over" and then add it to your "inside" when you feel you are making progress.

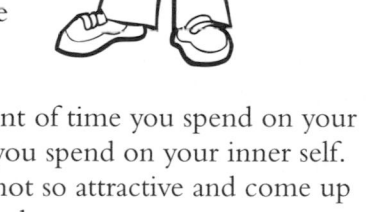

Older child: Compare the amount of time you spend on your outer appearance to the time you spend on your inner self. Pick one inner quality that is not so attractive and come up with ways to better yourself in that area.

Parenting Tip:
Reinforce the inner beauty of the child by tempering external compliments with internal compliments.

Related topic: Self-respect

BRAGGING

> **brag - v.** To talk in a boastful way about how good you are at something.
> **boast - v.** To talk proudly about what you can do or what you own in order to impress people.

Jeremiah 9:23–24

This is what the LORD says: "*Let not the wise man boast of his wisdom or the strong man boast of his strength or the rich man boast of his riches, but let him who boasts boast about this: that he understands and knows me, that I am the LORD, who exercises kindness, justice and righteousness on earth*, for in these I delight," declares the LORD.

Matthew 6:2a

"So when you give to the needy, do not announce it with trumpets, as the hypocrites do in the synagogues and on the streets, to be honored by men."

2 Corinthians 11:30

If I must boast, I will boast of the things that show my weakness.

Ephesians 2:8–9

For it is by grace you have been saved, through faith—and this not from yourselves, it is the gift of God—not by works, so that no one can boast.

James 4:16

As it is, you boast and brag. All such boasting is evil.

See also: 2 Corinthians 12:7–10; James 3:5

Discussion:
What is the difference between being proud of yourself and bragging? See definitions of brag and boast.

Read Matthew 6:2a for an example of bragging.

Think of a time when someone you know was bragging.

- ◆ How did it make you feel?
- ◆ What did it make you think of that person?

Think of a time when you bragged.

- ◆ How do you think it made others feel?
- ◆ What is something good you could do in place of bragging about yourself? See Take Action.

Read Jeremiah 9:23–24 and discuss what it says about boasting.

Read 2 Corinthians 11:30.

- ◆ Why would you want to boast about your weaknesses?
- ◆ Look up and read 2 Corinthians 12:7–10.

Take Action:
The next time you feel like bragging about yourself do the following instead. Find a way to lift someone else up by complimenting him. In front of your friends or family, pick something nonmaterial you admire about one of them and tell the others why you admire that person.

- ◆ How would doing that make the other person feel?
- ◆ How would it make you feel?
- ◆ Weigh the feeling you would gain from complimenting the other person against bragging about yourself. How do they compare?

Related topics: Pride; Conceitedness

CHANGE

change - v. To become different or to make different. *We changed the furniture in the living room.*

Psalm 55:19

God, who is enthroned forever, will hear them and afflict them—men who never change their ways and have no fear of God.

Ecclesiastes 3:1–2

There is a time for everything, and a season for every activity under heaven: a time to be born and a time to die, a time to plant and a time to uproot.

Philippians 4:12

I know what it is to be in need, and I know what it is to have plenty. I have learned the secret of being content in any and every situation, whether well fed or hungry, whether living in plenty or in want.

Hebrews 13:8

Jesus Christ is the same yesterday and today and forever.

Discussion:

What are some changes you have experienced in your life (moving, new school, physical changes, new baby in the family, death of a loved one, etc.)?

Is change normal? What does Ecclesiastes 3:1–2 say about change?

Who can you count on never changing? Read Hebrews 13:8.

Is Christ your stability and foundation in this world of change? Reference: Salvation.

Is there something about yourself or your situation that you wish you could change but over which you have no power? Read Philippians 4:12.

What could you be working on changing to make yourself a better person?

Take Action:

Timeline:

Following the example below, illustrate and/or write a timeline of your life.

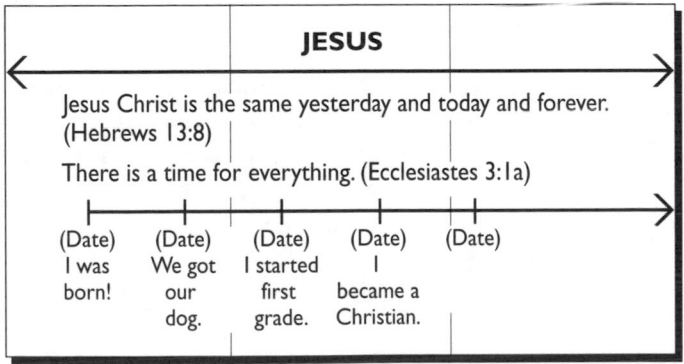

	JESUS		

Jesus Christ is the same yesterday and today and forever. (Hebrews 13:8)

There is a time for everything. (Ecclesiastes 3:1a)

| (Date) I was born! | (Date) We got our dog. | (Date) I started first grade. | (Date) I became a Christian. | (Date) |

CHARACTER

 **character - n.** Your **character** is what sort of person you are.

Ruth 3:11b
"All my fellow townsmen know that you are a woman of noble character."

Proverbs 31:10
A wife of noble character who can find? She is worth far more than rubies.

Luke 2:52
And Jesus grew in wisdom and stature and in favor with God and men.

Acts 17:11
Now the Bereans were of more noble character than the Thessalonians, for they received the message with great eagerness and examined the Scriptures every day to see if what Paul said was true.

Romans 5:3–5
Not only so, but we also rejoice in our sufferings, because we know that suffering produces perseverance; perseverance, character; and character, hope. And hope does not disappoint us, because God has poured out his love into our hearts by the Holy Spirit, whom He has given us.

1 Corinthians 15:33
Do not be misled: "Bad company corrupts good character."

Discussion:

Discuss the meaning of character. How a person daily lives out these topics is a reflection of his character.

How valuable is good character? Read Proverbs 31:10.

Do others notice your character? Read Ruth 3:11b.

On a scale of 1–10, rate how important it is that your friends have good character. Read 1 Corinthians 15:33.

Make a T-chart and identify qualities of friends with:

Weak Character	Good Character
Negative Influence	Positive Influence
Lack of Sense of Right Vs. Wrong	Good Sense of Right Vs. Wrong
Disrespectful	Respectful

- ◆ Which of your friends fall into which category?
- ◆ With whom should you be spending time?
- ◆ Would your friends think you have good character?

Take Action:
Character Building Plan:
Study a different topic each week and . . .

- ➤ Memorize one of the verses.
- ➤ Think carefully about the discussion questions.
- ➤ Follow through by taking action on God's word.

CHARITY

 **charity - n. 1.** An organization that raises money to help people in need. **2.** Money or other help that is given to people in need.

Matthew 6:2

"*So when you give to the needy, do not announce it with trumpets,* as the hypocrites do in the synagogues and on the streets, to be honored by men. I tell you the truth, they have received their reward in full."

Luke 12:33

"Sell your possessions and *give to the poor.* Provide purses for yourselves that will not wear out, a treasure in heaven that will not be exhausted, where no thief comes near and no moth destroys."

Acts 9:36

In Joppa there was a disciple named Tabitha (which, when translated, is Dorcas), who was always doing good and helping the poor.

Acts 10:2

He and all his family were devout and God-fearing; he gave generously to those in need and prayed to God regularly.

2 Corinthians 9:6

Remember this: Whoever sows sparingly will also reap sparingly, and whoever sows generously will also reap generously.

Discussion:
List as many different charities as you can and discuss how each helps people.

Read and discuss what the Bible has to say about charity in Luke 12:33; Matthew 6:2; and 2 Corinthians 9:6.

Can you think of anyone who is always willing to give of his time or money to help those in need?

- ◆ Read about two people in the Bible who are characterized that way in Acts 9:36 and Acts 10:2.
- ◆ Would people characterize you as a selfish or charitable (giving) person? Why?

Take Action:
1. *Give the Matthew 6:2 Way:* Do you know a person or family that needs assistance in a particular way? Find a way to secretively help them. Do not talk about it to anyone outside your family. Discuss the satisfaction you gained without "announcing" your good deeds to the recipients or others.

2. Determine a way that you can be charitable. Pick one of the following or think of your own idea:

- ➤ Go through your house and find items you no longer need. Give these items to the needy.
- ➤ Collect food for a food pantry.
- ➤ Volunteer at a food pantry or a soup kitchen.
- ➤ Help an elderly person with household chores.
- ➤ Pick any charity, ministry, or community project and find out how you can help support it.

Related topics: Giving; Ministry

CHEERFULNESS

cheerful - adj. Happy and lively.

Psalm 68:3

But may the righteous be glad and rejoice before God; may they be happy and joyful.

Proverbs 15:13

A happy heart makes the face cheerful, but heartache crushes the spirit.

Proverbs 15:15b

The cheerful heart has a continual feast.

Proverbs 15:30a

A cheerful look brings joy to the heart.

Proverbs 17:22

A cheerful heart is good medicine, but a crushed spirit dries up the bones.

2 Corinthians 9:7

Each man should give what he has decided in his heart to give, not reluctantly or under compulsion, for God loves a cheerful giver.

 **Discussion:**
Who do you know that is a cheery person?

- Do you think he has a cheerful heart?
- Do you think he enjoys life?
- Is he fun to be around? Why or why not?

Who do you know that is usually unhappy or grumpy?

- Do you think he has a cheerful heart?
- Do you think he enjoys life?
- Is he fun to be around? Why or why not?

What do you think Proverbs 15:15b means?

You always have a *choice* to look at the good or bad side of circumstances. Make a habit of looking at the bright side. Focusing on the good will help you maintain a cheerful heart and make you more pleasant to be around.

 **Take Action:**
1. Smile. It is the simplest way to bring cheer into the lives of others. Read Proverbs 15:30.

2. Give yourself some Proverbs 17:22 medicine. What can you do to help your heart be cheerful? Can you choose to have a more cheerful attitude?

3. Are you a cheerful giver? Read 2 Corinthians 9:7.
This week, have a cheerful attitude as you give your tithe to the church. Focus on the good your contribution will bring to the body of Christ.

4. Are you cheerful when you come before God in your daily quiet time or when you attend church? Practice going before God with the attitude of Psalm 68:3.

Related topic: Joyfulness

CHOICES

choose - v. 1. To pick out one person or thing from several. **2.** If you **choose** to do something, you decide to do it.

Joshua 24:15
"But if serving the LORD seems undesirable to you, then choose for yourselves this day whom you will serve, whether the gods your forefathers served beyond the River, or the gods of the Amorites, in whose land you are living. But as for me and my household, we will serve the LORD."

Proverbs 3:5–6
Trust in the LORD with all your heart and lean not on your own understanding; in all your ways acknowledge him, and he will make your paths straight.

Proverbs 3:31–32
Do not envy a violent man or choose any of his ways, for the LORD detests a perverse man but takes the upright into his confidence.

Proverbs 8:10–11
Choose my instruction instead of silver, knowledge rather than choice gold, for wisdom is more precious than rubies, and nothing you desire can compare with her.

Ephesians 5:15–17
Be very careful, then, how you live—not as unwise but as wise, making the most of every opportunity, because the days are evil. Therefore do not be foolish, but understand what the Lord's will is.

James 4:17
Anyone, then, who knows the good he ought to do and doesn't do it, sins.

 **Discussion:**
Discuss a recent choice or decision you made.

- How did you go about making your final decision?
- Did you think about it for a while? Discuss it with some friends or family members? Seek guidance? Stress about it?

Are everyday, little choices less important than big decisions?[1] Why?

What should you use as your guide when making a little or big decision?[2] Read Proverbs 3:5–6; Proverbs 8:10–11; and James 4:17.

What is the most important choice or decision you will ever make? Read Joshua 24:15 and reference: Salvation.

 **Take Action:**
1. Each morning, ask God to help you make good choices throughout the day (what you say, what you do, etc.).

2. When a big decision arises, try making a pro/con list and praying over it.

 **Parenting Tip:**
Sometimes, instead of lecturing your child when he has done something wrong, let him do the talking. For example, ask "Was that a good choice or bad choice?" Then, ask "Why?" Do not accept "I don't know" as an answer. Require the child to think for himself and explain the reason.

Related topic: Discernment

---

1. Not in most cases, since all the small choices make up a person's character. What you do defines who you are.
2. "WWJD" (What Would Jesus Do?).

COMFORT

 **comfort - v.** To make someone feel less worried or upset. *We comforted the lost child.*

Psalm 119:50
My comfort in my suffering is this: Your promise preserves my life.

Psalm 119:76–77
May your unfailing love be my comfort, according to your promise to your servant. Let your compassion come to me that I may live, for your law is my delight.

Matthew 5:4
"Blessed are those who mourn, for they will be comforted."

Romans 8:28
And we know that in all things God works for the good of those who love him, who have been called according to his purpose.

2 Corinthians 1:3–4
Praise be to the God and Father of our Lord Jesus Christ, the Father of compassion and the *God of all comfort, who comforts us in all our troubles, so that we can comfort those in any trouble* with the comfort we ourselves have received from God.

2 Corinthians 7:6–7a
But God, who comforts the downcast, comforted us by the coming of Titus, and not only by his coming but also by the comfort you had given him.

Discussion:
What are some things that comfort you when you are upset?

- ◆ Can you always depend on those things to comfort you?
- ◆ How is God better than those things?[1]

Read 2 Corinthians 1:3–4.

- ◆ Which troubles can you bring to God?
- ◆ What can you do for others as a result of God's blessing you with His comfort?

Take Action:
1. Do you need comforting? Follow 2 Corinthians 1:3–4. Give God your troubles in prayer and ask Him to send His comfort. Praise Him for being the "God of all comfort."

2. Be like Titus, whom God used to comfort others (see 2 Corinthians 7:6–7a). Pick someone who you know needs comforting and take action on one or more of these ideas to help comfort him.

- ➤ Give a listening ear.
- ➤ Send a card.
- ➤ Be a shoulder to cry on.
- ➤ Take flowers, cookies, etc.
- ➤ Share Christ with him.
- ➤ Share helpful and encouraging verses with him.
- ➤ Use an idea that someone used to comfort you.
- ➤ Think of your own ideas.

Related topics: Sadness; Suffering

1. He's always there—anytime, anyplace. He can hear and listen to you. He cares about you more than anyone else does. He wants to comfort you. See 2 Corinthians 1:3–4.

COMMITMENT

 **commit - v.** If you **commit** yourself to something, you promise that you will do it or support it.

Numbers 30:1b–2
"This is what the LORD commands: *When a man makes a vow to the Lord or takes an oath to obligate himself by a pledge, he must not break his word but must do everything he said.*"

Psalm 37:5–6
Commit your way to the LORD; trust in him and he will do this: He will make your righteousness shine like the dawn, the justice of your cause like the noonday sun.

Ecclesiastes 5:5
It is better not to vow than to make a vow and not fulfill it.

Matthew 5:37
"*Simply let your 'Yes' be 'Yes,' and your 'No,' 'No';* anything beyond this comes from the evil one."

1 Corinthians 15:58
Therefore, my dear brothers, stand firm. Let nothing move you. Always give yourselves fully to the work of the Lord, because you know that your labor in the Lord is not in vain.

Galatians 6:9
Let us not become weary in doing good, for at the proper time we will reap a harvest if we do not give up.

See also: Genesis 21:1–2; Proverbs 16:3; 1 Peter 4:19

Discussion:
What are the current commitments you have in your life (i.e., ball team, part in a play, attend a friend's party)?

◆ What would happen if you quit or did not keep your commitment to these things?

Pretend you have a soccer game and you decided you would rather stay home.

◆ How would your team members feel?

◆ What if everybody took the commitment of being on the team that lightly?

Pretend you have promised to attend a friend's birthday party. Then, you get another party invitation for the same time that sounds like more fun.

◆ What should you do?

◆ Why? Read Matthew 5:37 and Galatians 6:9.

What should your number one commitment be?

◆ Read Psalm 37:5–6 and 1 Corinthians 15:58.

◆ What does God promise in Psalm 37:5–6 He will do if you commit yourself to Him and trust in Him?

Take Action:
Live by Ecclesiastes 5:5:
Think before you speak! Before you promise or commit to anything, pray and think through it carefully.

Parenting Tip:
Once your child has committed or promised to do something, do not let him back down (unless the commitment is completely unreasonable) even if it would be easier on you and the child. He must learn that his words hold value. Read Numbers 30:1–2. This also applies to you as a parent.

COMPASSION

 **compassion - n.** A feeling of sympathy for and a desire to help someone who is suffering.

Psalm 103:13
As a father has compassion on his children, so the LORD has compassion on those who fear him.

Psalm 145:8–9
The LORD is gracious and compassionate, slow to anger and rich in love. *The LORD is good to all; he has compassion on all he has made.*

Matthew 15:32
Jesus called his disciples to him and said, "I have compassion for these people; they have already been with me three days and have nothing to eat. I do not want to send them away hungry, or they may collapse on the way."

Ephesians 4:32
Be kind and compassionate to one another, forgiving each other, just as in Christ God forgave you.

Colossians 3:12
Therefore, as God's chosen people, holy and dearly loved, clothe yourselves with compassion, kindness, humility, gentleness and patience.

1 Peter 3:8
Finally, all of you, live in harmony with one another; be sympathetic, love as brothers, be compassionate and humble.

See also: Matthew 9:36; 14:14

 **Discussion:**
Read an example of Jesus' compassion in Matthew 15:32.

Think of a time when someone showed you compassion when you were down or needed help.

- ♦ How did he help you?
- ♦ How did his compassion make you feel?
- ♦ Did that person have to do or say what he did?

 **Take Action:**
"Clothe yourselves with compassion" (Colossians 3:12).

Examples:

- ➤ *Parent:* Save money each month to help sponsor a child through a hunger relief program. Your child can write letters or draw pictures to send to the sponsor child and study the area in which the child lives.
- ➤ *Parent:* In your car, keep bottles of water and nonperishable food items such as packages of peanut-butter crackers to give to people who hold signs at stoplights that say "Will work for food." You may also want to give them a tract that tells the plan of salvation.
- ➤ Visit a nursing home and take homemade gifts.
- ➤ Think of a way to show compassion to someone at school this week.

Parenting Tip:
Teaching your child to show compassion to those in need is an excellent way to help her keep a balanced perspective on the difference between want and need.

COMPETITION

competition - n. A situation in which two or more people are trying to get the same thing. *There was a lot of competition for awards at school.*

Ecclesiastes 4:4
And I saw that all labor and all achievement spring from man's envy of his neighbor. This too is meaningless, a chasing after the wind.

Mark 9:33–35
They came to Capernaum. When he was in the house, he asked them, "What were you arguing about on the road?" But they kept quiet because on the way they had argued about who was the greatest. Sitting down, Jesus called the Twelve and said, "If anyone wants to be first, he must be the very last, and the servant of all."

Philippians 2:3
Do nothing out of selfish ambition or vain conceit, but in humility consider others better than yourselves.

2 Timothy 2:5
Similarly, if anyone competes as an athlete, he does not receive the victor's crown unless he competes according to the rules.

 **Discussion:**
Are you competitive in sports and games?

◆ Is it OK to be competitive?[1]

◆ How should one compete?[2] Read 2 Timothy 2:5.

◆ How should you act when someone else wins?

Are you competitive in the areas of looks, siblings, possessions, or grades? Read Philippians 2:3.

Discuss a time when you were motivated to compete because of jealousy.

◆ Read Ecclesiastes 4:4.

◆ Why is the kind of competition mentioned in Ecclesiastes 4:4 described as "meaningless, a chasing after the wind"? Look up and read Matthew 6:19–21 to help you answer this question.

How often do you find yourself saying, "Me first!" or, "That's not fair!"? Read Mark 9:33–35 to see how Jesus responded to a similar situation.

Take Action:
Make a "Focus Jar":
Parent: Write the following three challenges on slips of paper and put them in a container. Let the child draw one and focus on it for several days. Discuss the child's experiences with the challenge at the end of each day.

◆ Compliment those who do better than you.

◆ Encourage someone who doesn't do as well as you.

◆ Whenever you see something that someone has that you want, think, *I don't have that, but I do have ___, for which I am thankful.*

---

1. Yes, but the important thing to remember is that it's not whether you win or lose, but how you play the game.
2. Fairly, according to the rules.

COMPLAINING

> **complain - v. 1.** To say that you are unhappy about something. *Bev always complains about the heat in the summer.* **2.** To report, or to make an accusation. *We complained to the police about the robbery.*

Numbers 11:4–6

The rabble with them began to crave other food, and again the Israelites started wailing and said, "If only we had meat to eat! We remember the fish we ate in Egypt at no cost—also the cucumbers, melons, leeks, onions and garlic. But now we have lost our appetite; we never see anything but this manna!"

1 Corinthians 10:10a

And do not grumble, as some of them did.

Philippians 2:14–16

Do everything without complaining or arguing, so that you may become blameless and pure, children of God without fault in a crooked and depraved generation, in which you shine like stars in the universe as you hold out the word of life—in order that I may boast on the day of Christ that I did not run or labor for nothing.

Jude 16

These men are grumblers and faultfinders; they follow their own evil desires; they boast about themselves and flatter others for their own advantage.

See also: Numbers 21:4–7; Lamentations 3:39

Discussion:

What is the point of complaining? Discuss the two types of complaining given in the definition.

Read Philippians 2:14–16. To which type of complaining do you think is being referred?

Read how ungrateful the Israelites were in Numbers 11:4–6 when they complained to God, even though He had kept them alive by giving them manna from heaven and was leading them to the Promised Land.

- ◆ Do you ever sound like the Israelites?

Take Action:

1. Keep a tally of each time you complain. See if you can decrease your daily totals this week.

2. *Parent:* Help your child think through the following list when he complains. Challenge the child to try to catch you in the act of complaining and help you think through the list.

- ➤ Will complaining help the situation?
- ➤ Is there a way I can help make the situation better for others and myself?
- ➤ Could I say something positive to offset my desire to complain?
- ➤ Should I just keep my mouth shut? Remember the old saying, "If you can't say anything nice, don't say anything at all."

Parenting Tip:

Whining is closely related to complaining. Make it clear that whining and complaining will not be tolerated and teach your child more appropriate ways of expressing himself.

Related topic: Contentment

COMPROMISE

> **compromise - 1. v.** To agree to accept something that is not exactly what you wanted. **2. n.** An agreement that is reached after people with opposing views each give up some of their demands.

Ecclesiastes 4:9

Two are better than one, because they have a good return for their work.

Acts 20:35b

"It is more blessed to give than to receive."

1 Corinthians 1:10

I appeal to you, brothers, in the name of our Lord Jesus Christ, that all of you agree with one another so that there may be no divisions among you and that you may be perfectly united in mind and thought.

Compromising Standards

Proverbs 25:26 (NLT)

If the godly compromise with the wicked, it is like polluting a fountain or muddying a spring.

Romans 12:2

Do not conform any longer to the pattern of this world, but be transformed by the renewing of your mind. Then you will be able to test and approve what God's will is—his good, pleasing and perfect will.

1 Corinthians 15:33

Do not be misled: "Bad company corrupts good character."

See also: Exodus 34:12; 2 Corinthians 6:14

Discussion:
Discuss the following scenarios:
Younger child: Jenny wants you to come over to play with her new game. You want Jenny to come over to play in your backyard. How could you and Jenny compromise?

Older child: You want to stay out later than your parents want you to after a school dance. How could you compromise?

- ◆ Possible compromise: Stay out until the time your parents want you to be home and arrange for a sleepover at your house for friends of the same gender for the rest of the night.

Discuss how compromise is beneficial. Read 1 Corinthians 1:10; Acts 20:35b; and Ecclesiastes 4:9.

Compromising standards:
In general, compromise is beneficial. However:

- ◆ Can you think of some examples when compromising would be bad?
- ◆ Read Proverbs 25:26 and 1 Corinthians 15:33 and relate your examples to these verses.
- ◆ How does Romans 12:2 say you can avoid compromising your standards?

Take Action:
Younger child: Cut out a smiley face and a sad face. Give the child an example of a good compromise or a bad compromise (i.e., compromising standards). Have the child respond by holding up the face that best represents the compromise, explain why, and try to come up with a related example for the face that is left.

Older child: Are you currently at odds with anyone over an issue? Brainstorm ways a compromise could be made to resolve the situation.

CONCEITEDNESS

 **conceited - adj.** If you are **conceited,** you are too proud of yourself and what you can do.

Jeremiah 13:15
Hear and pay attention, do not be arrogant, for the LORD has spoken.

Romans 12:3
For by the grace given me I say to every one of you: Do not think of yourself more highly than you ought, but rather think of yourself with sober judgment, in accordance with the measure of faith God has given you.

Romans 12:16b
Do not be proud, but be willing to associate with people of low position. *Do not be conceited.*

2 Corinthians 3:5
Not that we are competent in ourselves to claim anything for ourselves, but our competence comes from God.

2 Corinthians 12:7
To keep me from becoming conceited because of these surpassingly great revelations, there was given me a thorn in my flesh, a messenger of Satan, to torment me.

Galatians 5:26
Let us not become conceited, provoking and envying each other.

See also: 1 Timothy 6:17

 **Discussion:**
Can you feel that you are special without being conceited or snobby?

♦ How can you balance the two?[1]

Go to the library and read *Yertle the Turtle,* by Dr. Seuss.

♦ How was Yertle conceited?[2] Read Romans 12:16b.

♦ Read 2 Corinthians 12:7. What was Yertle's "thorn in his flesh" that kept him from becoming more conceited?

How does this story relate to you?

♦ Is there anyone you "step on" to get what you want?

♦ Is there anyone you have been putting down or thinking yourself better than? See Galatians 5:26.

♦ Have you been snobby about a particular thing you do well? Read Jeremiah 13:15.

♦ Do you have a "thorn in your flesh"? 2 Corinthians 12:7.

Have you been a victim of someone else's conceitedness? Look up and read Psalm 119:21 and Psalm 119:51.

Take Action:
1. Take time to go to the library. See Discussion.

2. Consider your responses to the discussion questions. What specifically will you do to positively change your thinking and actions in the area of conceitedness? Reference: Humility.

Parenting Tip:
Storybooks can be excellent teaching tools. Look for life-application lessons as you read stories to your child and take the opportunity for discussion.

---

1. It is healthy to feel self-confident and special. However, these feelings should not be taken to the point where you are thinking too highly of yourself (Romans 12:3) and looking down on others.
2. He was only thinking about himself. He did not care about the turtles under him and would not listen to them. He thought he was better than the others.

CONFIDENCE

 **confident - adj. 1.** Having a strong belief in your own abilities. **2.** Certain that things will happen in the way you want. *I am confident that I will pass the test.*

Proverbs 3:25
Have no fear of sudden disaster or of the ruin that overtakes the wicked, for the LORD will be your confidence and will keep your foot from being snared.

Jeremiah 17:7
"But blessed is the man who trusts in the LORD, whose confidence is in him."

Philippians 4:13
I can do everything through him who gives me strength.

Hebrews 4:16
Let us then approach the throne of grace with confidence, so that we may receive mercy and find grace to help us in our time of need.

Hebrews 10:35–36
So do not throw away your confidence; it will be richly rewarded. You need to persevere so that when you have done the will of God, you will receive what he has promised.

Hebrews 13:6
So we say with confidence, "The Lord is my helper; I will not be afraid. What can man do to me?"

See also: Psalms 27:1; 71:5; 118:8; Romans 8:31

Discussion:
Is there something now and/or in the past about which you have felt a lack of confidence?

◆ Read the following confidence builders:

Proverbs 3:25; Philippians 4:13; Hebrews 4:16; Hebrews 10:35–36; and Hebrews 13:6.

In whom is your utmost confidence?

◆ Who will never fail you? Read Jeremiah 17.7 and Hebrews 13:6.

Take Action:
1. Memorize the verse that gives you the most confidence so you will have it on your heart when you need it.

2. Rent the classic movie, *The Sound of Music,* and watch for and discuss the song "I Have Confidence," sung by the character Maria. It is near the beginning of the movie when Maria leaves the abbey to become a governess.

Parenting Tip:
Build confidence in your child and encourage him by frequently quoting the following verse to him:

"I have great confidence in you; I take great pride in you. I am greatly encouraged; in all our troubles my joy knows no bounds" (2 Corinthians 7:4).

CONFORMITY

> **conform - v. 1.** If you **conform,** you behave in the same way as everyone else or in a way that is expected of you. **2.** If something **conforms** to a rule or law, it does what the rule or law requires. *All these toys conform to strict safety regulations.*

Joshua 24:15
"But if serving the LORD seems undesirable to you, then *choose for yourselves this day whom you will serve,* whether the gods your forefathers served beyond the River, or the gods of the Amorites, in whose land you are living. *But as for me and my household, we will serve the LORD.*"

Psalm 1:1
Blessed is the man who does not walk in the counsel of the wicked or stand in the way of sinners or sit in the seat of mockers.

Romans 12:2
Do not conform any longer to the pattern of this world, but be transformed by the renewing of your mind. Then you will be able to test and approve what God's will is—his good, pleasing and perfect will.

James 4:17
Anyone, then, who knows the good he ought to do and doesn't do it, sins.

1 Peter 1:14
As obedient children, do not conform to the evil desires you had when you lived in ignorance.

🗣 Discussion:
Do you have friends who expect you to conform to negative behavior? Give examples.

◆ Read Psalm 1:1 and James 4:17.

Read Joshua 24:15. Whom will you choose to serve? God? Friends? Self?

Discuss the results of conforming to bad behavior.

Discuss the blessings of conforming to the Lord.

🏃 Take Action:
Parent: Think about "the renewing of your (child's) mind." Are you consistently providing opportunities for him to study and learn more about God at home and at church? As Romans 12:2 teaches, helping your child renew his mind is a key factor in him learning to not conform to the world. What can you do this week to take action in this important area? Make a list and determine to follow through with at least one idea.

💡 Parenting Tip:
Peer pressure is the main way children are tempted to conform to the world. Discuss peer pressure with your child and try to discern which areas might be a struggle for him. Encourage your child to be proud of his individuality and high moral standards. Help him understand that God will give him the strength to stand firm and reward his determination. Look up 1 Corinthians 10:12–13 and Galatians 6:9.

Related topics: Peer Pressure; Temptation

CONTENTMENT

content - adj. Happy and satisfied.

Ecclesiastes 4:8
There was a man all alone; he had neither son nor brother. There was no end to his toil, yet his eyes were not content with his wealth. "For whom am I toiling," he asked, "and why am I depriving myself of enjoyment?" This too is meaningless—a miserable business!

Philippians 4:12
I know what it is to be in need, and I know what it is to have plenty. I have learned the secret of being content in any and every situation, whether well fed or hungry, whether living in plenty or in want.

1 Timothy 6:6–8
But godliness with contentment is great gain. For we brought nothing into the world, and we can take nothing out of it. But if we have food and clothing, we will be content with that.

Hebrews 13:5
Keep your lives free from the love of money and *be content with what you have,* because God has said, "Never will I leave you; never will I forsake you."

Discussion:
Put a glass filled halfway in front of your child.
Discuss the question, "Is the glass half-full or half-empty?"

Who or what determines how content you are?

- Read Philippians 4:12.
- Point out that contentment is a choice and it all depends on which side of the glass your child picks for his focus. His attitudes and actions will reflect his choice.

What is something you have really been wanting? Can you be content, even if you never get it? Read 1 Timothy 6:6–8 and Hebrews 13:5.

Read about a wealthy man in Ecclesiastes 4:8 who realized that his discontent and greed had led to his unhappiness.

Take Action:
1. Learn the hymn "Count Your Blessings." It is a wonderful song to know by heart so that you can recall it anytime you want to rebuild or express the contentment in your heart.

2. Literally count your blessings. See how long of a list you can make of blessings in your life. Reflect on the list and reevaluate your level of contentment.

Parenting Tip:
Think about the times in your life when you struggled with being content. Share how you overcame discontent, or not, and what you learned from it.

Related topics: Greed; Money

COOPERATION

 **cooperate - v.** To work together.

Exodus 23:5

"If you see the donkey of someone who hates you fallen down under its load, do not leave it there; be sure you help him with it."

2 Chronicles 2:8–9

"Send me also cedar, pine and algum logs from Lebanon, for I know that your men are skilled in cutting timber there. My men will work with yours to provide me with plenty of lumber, because the temple I build must be large and magnificent."

Ecclesiastes 4:9–12

Two are better than one, because they have a good return for their work: If one falls down, his friend can help him up. But pity the man who falls and has no one to help him up! Also, if two lie down together, they will keep warm. But how can one keep warm alone? Though one may be overpowered, two can defend themselves. A cord of three strands is not quickly broken.

Luke 5:6–7 (For context, start with verse 4.)

When they had done so, they caught such a large number of fish that their nets began to break. So they signaled their partners in the other boat to come and help them, and they came and filled both boats so full that they began to sink.

 **Discussion:**
Discuss examples of cooperation that are specific to your life and read the biblical examples found in Luke 5:6–7 and 2 Chronicles 2:8–9.

Why is cooperation so important? Read Ecclesiastes 4:9–12.

Pretend that someone you do not like or who does not like you accidentally spilled everything out of his backpack in the hallway at school.

- ◆ What would you do?
- ◆ Read Exodus 23:5.

Take Action:
Parent: Plan a family activity that will prove that cooperation can be effective and fun.

Example:
The house is a mess and needs straightening and cleaning. Turn on some music and work together until the house is clean. Add up the time it took for each person to complete his or her share. Then, spend that amount of time going to the park, watching a movie, or being involved in some other activity the whole family can enjoy. Discuss how somebody would still be working on the house if there had not been cooperation.

Take this concept and apply it to situations specific to your family. Emphasize the impact that cooperation has on the project.

Related topics: Respect; Sharing

COURAGE

 **courage - n.** Bravery, or fearlessness.

Psalm 4:8
I will lie down and sleep in peace, for you alone, O LORD, make me dwell in safety.

Psalm 27:1
The LORD is my light and my salvation—whom shall I fear? The LORD is the stronghold of my life—of whom shall I be afraid?

Psalm 46:1–2a
God is our refuge and strength, an ever-present help in trouble. Therefore we will not fear.

Isaiah 41:13
"For I am the LORD, your God, who takes hold of your right hand and says to you, Do not fear; I will help you."

Philippians 4:13
I can do everything through him who gives me strength.

2 Timothy 1:7
For God did not give us a spirit of timidity, but a spirit of power, of love and of self-discipline.

Hebrews 13:6
So we say with confidence, "*The Lord is my helper; I will not be afraid.* What can man do to me?"

See also: Psalms 23; 91:9–11; Isaiah 41:10

 **Discussion:**
What are some things of which you are afraid?

◆ What does God say about fear and being afraid? Read Psalm 27:1; Psalm 46:1–2a; and Isaiah 41:13.

◆ Take time right now to thank God for being bigger than all of your fears.

What are some things that are hard for you and for which you need courage (i.e., talking to a new person in your class, standing up for what is right, performing at a recital, etc.)?

◆ What does God say about courage? Read Philippians 4:13; 2 Timothy 1:7; and Hebrews 13:6.

 **Take Action:**
1. Learn Philippians 4:13 by putting the words to "Row, Row, Row Your Boat." (Tip: Repeat the verse twice to complete the melody.)

2. Chant Philippians 4:13, out loud or in your head, when you are needing motivation to be courageous. For example: "I can do" clap, clap "everything" clap, clap "through Him" clap, clap "who gives me strength." clap, clap — Repeat . . .

3. Make a bookmark for your Bible. Write "Courage!" at the top of the bookmark. Underneath write, "When I am afraid, read Psalm 46:1–3!" Decorate the bookmark and mark Psalm 46:1–3. The bookmark will serve as a reminder of where to look the next time you are afraid and need courage.

Parenting Tip:
Putting Scripture to familiar melodies or chants is a wonderful way to help your child learn verses. The words will stick in his head for a lifetime and come to the rescue when most needed.

Related topic: Confidence

CRAFTY

> **crafty - adj.** A **crafty** person is skilled at
> tricking other people.

Genesis 3:1 (Read Genesis 2:15–3:34 for context.)
Now the serpent was more crafty than any of the wild animals
the LORD God had made. He said to the woman, "Did God
really say, 'You must not eat from any tree in the garden'?"

Job 5:12–13
"He thwarts the plans of the crafty, so that their hands achieve
no success. He catches the wise in their craftiness, and the
schemes of the wily are swept away."

Psalm 119:29
Keep me from deceitful ways; be gracious to me through your
law.

Proverbs 12:2
A good man obtains favor from the LORD, but *the LORD con-
demns a crafty man.*

Proverbs 14:17
A quick-tempered man does foolish things, and *a crafty man is
hated.*

See also: Psalm 64:5–8

 **Discussion:**
Discuss examples of craftiness.[1]

- ◆ Read Genesis 3 (only verse one is listed on the previous page).
- ◆ Discuss how the serpent was crafty.
- ◆ Warn your child that he may run across crafty people. For example: Another young person may try to sell you drugs and use reasonable sounding arguments to persuade you. He is being crafty like the snake.

What are the consequences of craftiness? Read Job 5:12–13 and Proverbs 14:17.

Read Proverbs 14:17. Why do you think a crafty man is hated?

Take Action:
Parent of younger child: If your child is prone to cheating, play a game where you, the parent, cheat throughout the entire game. When the child notices and objects, explain that you are cheating to prove the point of how it feels to be on the receiving end of craftiness.

Parent of older child: Reference the parenting tip and spend some quality time this week role-playing with your child.

Parenting Tip:
Peer pressure involves much craftiness. Preparing your child with ways to handle situations before they arise is half the battle. Arm your child with knowledge from role-playing, frank discussions, and an outlining of consequences; and he will be more likely to make a better decision when faced with the craftiness of peer pressure.

Related topic: Honesty

1. Cheating, dishonesty, conniving to get one's way, negatively tricking others, etc.

CRITICISM

 **criticize - v.** To tell someone what he or she has done wrong. **2.** To point out the good and bad parts in a book, movie, play, television program, etc.

Proverbs 11:17
A kind man benefits himself, but a cruel man brings trouble on himself.

Proverbs 15:31–32
He who listens to a life-giving rebuke will be at home among the wise. He who ignores discipline despises himself, but whoever heeds correction gains understanding.

Proverbs 27:6
Wounds from a friend can be trusted, but an enemy multiplies kisses.

Matthew 5:44
"But I tell you: Love your enemies and pray for those who persecute you."

Matthew 7:1–2
"Do not judge, or you too will be judged. For in the same way you judge others, you will be judged, and with the measure you use, it will be measured to you."

Luke 6:31
"Do to others as you would have them do to you."

Romans 14:10
You, then, why do you judge your brother? Or why do you look down on your brother? For we will all stand before God's judgment seat.

 **Discussion:**
Are you guilty of criticizing people's:

❖ clothes   ❖ looks   ❖ abilities

❖ habits   ❖ mannerisms   ❖ interests

Take the same list and turn it around on yourself. How would you feel if someone was as critical of you as you have been of others? Read Matthew 7:1–2 and Luke 6:31.

Sometimes a person criticizes in order to lift himself up in the eyes of those listening. Does that really do any good? Read Romans 14:10.

How can you deal with someone who is critical of you? Read Matthew 5.44.

Can criticism ever be positive?

◆ Read and discuss Proverbs 15:31–32 and 27:6.

◆ Discuss the term "constructive criticism."

 **Take Action:**
Think Before You Speak:

◆ Am I about to say something critical?

◆ Would I want someone saying something similar about me (Luke 6:31)?

◆ Is there a way I can be kind instead of cruel? (Proverbs 11:17)?

◆ Am I being critical of others simply to make myself feel better (Romans 14:10)?

When You Are Criticized, Think Before You React:

◆ Is there any truth to what was said (Proverbs 27:6)?

◆ Was the person trying to be helpful or hurtful?

CURSING

 **curse - v.** To swear.

Exodus 20:7

"You shall not misuse the name of the LORD your God, for the LORD will not hold anyone guiltless who misuses his name."

Leviticus 19:12

"Do not swear falsely by my name and so profane the name of your God. I am the LORD."

Psalm 19:14

May the words of my mouth and the meditation of my heart be pleasing in your sight, O LORD, my Rock and my Redeemer.

Ephesians 4:29

Do not let any unwholesome talk come out of your mouths, but only what is helpful for building others up according to their needs, that it may benefit those who listen.

Ephesians 5:4

Nor should there be obscenity, foolish talk or coarse joking, which are out of place, but rather thanksgiving.

James 3:10

Out of the same mouth come praise and cursing. My brothers, this should not be.

See also: Luke 6:45

Discussion:

Does cursing do any good? What phrases do you think Exodus 20:7 and Leviticus 19:12 might be talking about?[1]

Read Ephesians 4:29 and Ephesians 5:4. Think of some other things you can say in place of curse words.[2]

Take Action:

1. Do you have a problem with cursing? Ask family and friends to make a bleeping noise when you curse to remind you of what has come out of your mouth. The idea comes from the noise used when bad words are "bleeped" out on radio or television.

2. Does someone close to you curse frequently? Politely ask him not to do it when you are around. This request will positively influence him and make him rethink what comes out of his mouth.

If this person desires to quit his habit of cursing, ask if you can use the idea from number one to help.

3. Add the words of Psalm 19:14 to your prayer time.

Parenting Tip:

Do not say anything you would not want to hear your child saying. Your example is powerful.

1. "Oh, my God!" "I swear to God!" "Jesus!" "God!"
2. "Bummer!" "Oh, No!" "Rats!"

DEATH

death - n. The end of [physical] life.

Psalm 23:4
Even though I walk through the valley of the shadow of death, I will fear no evil, for you are with me; your rod and your staff, they comfort me.

Psalm 116:15
Precious in the sight of the LORD is the death of his saints.

Matthew 5:4
"Blessed are those who mourn, for they will be comforted."

Romans 6:23
For the wages of sin is death, but the gift of God is eternal life in Christ Jesus our Lord.

I Thessalonians 4:13–14
Brothers, we do not want you to be ignorant about those who fall asleep, or to grieve like the rest of men, who have no hope. We believe that Jesus died and rose again and so we believe that God will bring with Jesus those who have fallen asleep in him.

Revelation 21:4
"He will wipe every tear from their eyes. There will be no more death or mourning or crying or pain, for the old order of things has passed away."

See also: Proverbs 14:32; Jonah 2:7; John 5:24; 11:25–26; 14:2; 1 Corinthians 15:55; James 5:20

 **Discussion:**
What are the two main parts of a person?[1]

◆ Can anyone avoid physical death?

◆ Can anyone avoid spiritual death? How? Read Romans 6:23.

◆ What will happen to you when your physical body dies? Reference: Salvation.

Read the remaining verses and be comforted with what the Bible says about death.

 **Take Action:**
If someone close to the child has died:
1. Read and discuss Christian children's books that deal with loss and grief.

2. Make a memory book or box. Include written memories and special photographs.

3. Christian counseling may be a worthwhile investment.

Parenting Tips:
How deep you go into explaining death to your child depends on his age and maturity. Refer to your minister, children's minister, or related books for guidance.

Be honest with your child and acknowledge that death and grief are a natural part of life, but focus on the hope of eternal life through Jesus Christ.

Related topics: Comfort; Encouragement; Hope; Sadness; Salvation; Sympathy

---

1. Physical/spiritual and body/soul.

DISCERNMENT

 **discern - v.** To perceive or recognize clearly.

I Kings 3:9a (Read verses 7–14 for context.)
"So give your servant a discerning heart to govern your people and to distinguish between right and wrong."

Job 34:4
"Let us discern for ourselves what is right; let us learn together what is good."

Proverbs 3:21–24
My son, preserve sound judgment and discernment, do not let them out of your sight; they will be life for you, an ornament to grace your neck. Then you will go on your way in safety, and your foot will not stumble; when you lie down, you will not be afraid; when you lie down, your sleep will be sweet.

Proverbs 10:13
Wisdom is found on the lips of the discerning, but a rod is for the back of him who lacks judgment.

Philippians 1:9–11
And this is my prayer: that your love may abound more and more in knowledge and depth of insight, so that you may be able to discern what is best and may be pure and blameless until the day of Christ, filled with the fruit of righteousness that comes through Jesus Christ—to the glory and praise of God.

James 4:17
Anyone, then, who knows the good he ought to do and doesn't do it, sins.

See also: Joshua 1:8; Proverbs 28:11

Discussion:
Read 1 Kings 3:9a. What did King Solomon ask of God?

Why is discernment so important? Read Proverbs 3:21–24.

- *Younger child:* In simple terms, discernment is what helps you understand right from wrong and keeps you out of trouble.
- *Older child:* Try to relate the verse to your life.

What happens when you lack discernment?[1] See Proverbs 10:13.

- Discuss examples of what happened when you lacked discernment and when you showed discernment.

Read Job 34:4 and consider how you can show discernment in the following areas:

❖ Friends ❖ Music ❖ Internet ❖ Movies ❖ Other

Example: Friends

- Choose friends who have similar values and who will respect your standards
- Be willing to put your values ahead of your friendships in peer pressure situations.

Take Action:
Parent: Commit to praying Philippians 1:9–11 for your child on a regular basis.

Child: Follow King Solomon's example and ask God to help you discern right from wrong. Also, use the WWJD (What Would Jesus Do?) test.

Related topic: Judgment

---

1. You get yourself in trouble.

DISCIPLINE

 **discipline - n.** Control over the way that you or other people behave. *My aunt thinks my brother is too wild and needs more discipline.*

Proverbs 5:23
He will die for lack of discipline, led astray by his own great folly.

Proverbs 10:17
He who heeds discipline shows the way to life, but whoever ignores correction leads others astray.

Proverbs 29:17
Discipline your son, and he will give you peace; he will bring delight to your soul.

Hebrews 12:5b–11
"My son, do not make light of the Lord's discipline, and do not lose heart when he rebukes you, because the Lord disciplines those he loves, and he punishes everyone he accepts as a son." Endure hardship as discipline; God is treating you as sons. For what son is not disciplined by his father? If you are not disciplined (and everyone undergoes discipline), then you are illegitimate children and not true sons. Moreover, we have all had human fathers who disciplined us and we respected them for it. How much more should we submit to the Father of our spirits and live! Our fathers disciplined us for a little while as they thought best; but God disciplines us for our good, that we may share in his holiness. *No discipline seems pleasant at the time, but painful. Later on, however, it produces a harvest of righteousness and peace for those who have been trained by it.*

See also: Proverbs 1:7; 12:1; Revelation 3:19

 **Discussion:**
Think about all the bad things you've done that caused you to be disciplined.

- ◆ What do you think you'd be like if you were never disciplined? Why do you think it is important for me, your parent, to discipline you? Read Hebrews 12:5b–11.

Imagine that you began lying about things. If I, your parent, do not stop you by disciplining you, then people will begin to not trust you.

- ◆ Do you want your friends not to trust you?
- ◆ Do you want your family not to trust you?
- ◆ Can you see why I love you enough to discipline you?

Beware of your friends who ignore discipline. What does Proverbs 10:17 say these people do?

Take Action:
Memorize Hebrews 12:11.

Parenting Tips:
1. Read Proverbs 5:23 and Proverbs 29:17. Evaluate the discipline system you have set up in your household. What is working and what is not? Why? The harmony of your home and well-being of your child will depend on the application of this topic. Therefore, make sure you have a definitive and consistently applied system.

2. Anytime your child is upset about consequences, remind him that he put himself in that position.

Related topic: Obedience

DISCOURAGEMENT

 **discourage - 1. v.** If you **discourage** people from doing something, you persuade them not to do it. **2. adj.** If you are **discouraged,** you lose your enthusiasm or confidence.

Deuteronomy 31:8
"The LORD himself goes before you and will be with you; he will never leave you nor forsake you. Do not be afraid; *do not be discouraged."*

Joshua 1:9
"Have I not commanded you? Be strong and courageous. Do not be terrified; do not be discouraged, for the LORD your God will be with you wherever you go."

Nehemiah 6:9
They were all trying to frighten us, thinking, "Their hands will get too weak for the work, and it will not be completed." But I prayed, "Now strengthen my hands."

Psalm 31:24
Be strong and take heart, all you who hope in the LORD.

John 16:33
"I have told you these things, so that in me you may have peace. *In this world you will have trouble. But take heart! I have overcome the world."*

Colossians 3:21
Fathers, do not embitter your children, or they will become discouraged.

See also: Psalm 18:6; 2 Corinthians 1:3–4

 **Discuss:**
Discuss a time when you felt discouraged.

Nehemiah also had to fight discouragement. Read Nehemiah 6:9 and find out how he battled it.

What else does the Bible have to say about discouragement? Read Deuteronomy 31:8; Joshua 1:9; Psalm 31:24; and John 16:33.

Can discouraging others ever be a good thing? How?[1]

♦ List some examples of when it would be good to discourage others.

Take Action:
1. Study the topic Encouragement and learn how you can be encouraged and an encourager instead of discouraged and a discourager.

2. Predetermine to be a positive influence on your friends by helping discourage them when they want to behave badly. Role-play scenarios.

Example: Friends want you to do something you know is not right. You could say, "I think I'd rather go play some basketball. Anyone want to come with me?"

Parenting Tip:
Read Colossians 3:21. Think carefully: Are you embittering your child in any way? Be honest with yourself and decide how to better handle the relationship.

Related topics: Comfort; Encouragement

---

1. Yes, when people are about to make a bad choice or decision.

ENCOURAGEMENT

encourage - v. To give someone confidence by praising or supporting the person. *The teacher encouraged us to do our best.*

Deuteronomy 3:28
"But commission Joshua, and encourage and strengthen him, for he will lead this people across and will cause them to inherit the land that you will see."

Psalm 31:24
Be strong and take heart, all you who hope in the LORD.

Psalm 64:5
They encourage each other in evil plans, they talk about hiding their snares; they say, "Who will see them?"

Romans 15:4
For everything that was written in the past was written to teach us, so that through endurance and the encouragement of the Scriptures we might have hope.

2 Thessalonians 2:16
May our Lord Jesus Christ himself and God our Father, who loved us and by his grace gave us eternal encouragement and good hope, encourage your hearts and strengthen you in every good deed and word.

Hebrews 3:13
But encourage one another daily, as long as it is called Today, so that none of you may be hardened by sin's deceitfulness.

See also: Psalm 31:24; Isaiah 40:30–31; Romans 12:8; 1 Thessalonians 5:11

Discuss:
Think of a time when someone encouraged you. How did it make you feel? Did it help?

Who can you *always* look to for encouragement? Read 2 Thessalonians 2:16.

Where do Romans 15:4 and Hebrews 3:13 say you can find encouragement?

Why does Hebrews 3:13 emphasize encouragement?

Is encouragement always good? Read Psalm 64:5.
Beware of people who try to encourage you to do bad things.

Take Action:
1. "Encourage one another" (Hebrews 3:13). Who do you know that needs some encouragement? Do one of the following for him or come up with your own idea:

◆ Write a note of encouragement or draw a picture.

◆ Plan a visit or outing.

◆ Cook something special.

2. Do you need encouragement? Romans 15:4 says the Scriptures were given to us for this reason. Memorize a verse that is especially encouraging to you.

3. *Older child:* Deuteronomy 3:28 instructs the Israelites to encourage Joshua, their leader. Find out who the political representatives are in your area. Write and encourage them to stand up for what is morally right.

Related idea: Find a way to encourage your church leaders.

EXAMPLE

 **example - n. 1.** Something typical of a larger group of things. *The whale is an example of a mammal.* **2.** A model for others to follow. *Sandra is a good example for the rest of the class.*

Proverbs 20:11
Even a child is known by his actions, by whether his conduct is pure and right.

1 Corinthians 10:32a
Do not cause anyone to stumble.

1 Thessalonians 1:7–8a
And so you became a model to all the believers in Macedonia and Achaia. The Lord's message rang out from you not only in Macedonia and Achaia—your faith in God has become known everywhere.

1 Timothy 4:12
Don't let anyone look down on you because you are young, but set an example for the believers in speech, in life, in love, in faith and in purity.

Titus 2:7a
In everything set them an example by doing what is good.

1 Peter 2:12
Live such good lives among the pagans that, though they accuse you of doing wrong, they may see your good deeds and glorify God on the day he visits us.

1 Peter 2:21
To this you were called, because Christ suffered for you, leaving you an example, that you should follow in his steps.

EXAMPLE   79

 **Discussion:**
To whom are you an example?[1]

◆ How can you be an example to others? Read the verses.

Read Proverbs 20:11. What would people say about you in light of your actions?

What does 1 Corinthians 10:32a mean? Give examples.

Do you ever feel less significant because you are young? Read 1 Timothy 4:12.

Whose example should you strive to follow? Read 1 Peter 2:21.

Take Action:
WWJD? (What Would Jesus Do)?
Parent: First Peter 2:21 says we should look to Jesus as a good example. Tell your child to do the following things, adding your own ideas, and have him answer "yes" or "no" depending on what he thinks Jesus would do.

◆ Smoke a cigarette.   ◆ Complain about chores.

◆ Study hard for a test.   ◆ Call someone a bad name.

◆ Spend your tithe on a toy. ◆ Help clean up the house.

◆ Take money from Mom's purse without asking.

◆ Tell the truth about something you broke.

Parenting Tip:
Remember that you are the most important example to your child. Be careful not to do or say anything you would not want your child to do or say.

---

1. Friends, family, strangers, teachers, everyone.

FAIRNESS

> **fair - adj.** Reasonable and just, as in **fair** treatment. **adv.** By the rules. *Play fair!*

Ecclesiastes 7:14–15
When times are good, be happy; but when times are bad, consider: God has made the one as well as the other. Therefore, a man cannot discover anything about his future. In this meaningless life of mine I have seen both of these: a righteous man perishing in his righteousness, and a wicked man living long in his wickedness.

Luke 3:12–13
Tax collectors also came to be baptized. "Teacher," they asked, "what should we do?" "Don't collect any more than you are required to," he told them.

Luke 6:31
"Do to others as you would have them do to you."

John 16:33
"I have told you these things, so that in me you may have peace. In this world you will have trouble. But take heart! I have overcome the world."

2 Thessalonians 1:6
God is just: He will pay back trouble to those who trouble you.

2 Timothy 2:5
Similarly, if anyone competes as an athlete, he does not receive the victor's crown unless he competes according to the rules.

See also: Psalm 89:14; Proverbs 12:5; Micah 6:8; 1 John 1:9

Discussion:

What are some ways that you and your friends and/or siblings are fair and unfair with each other?

When someone treats you unfairly, does that give you a right to be unfair back to him? Why? Read Luke 6:31 and 2 Thessalonians 1:6.

In Luke 3:12–13, John the Baptist talks with the tax collectors who have been treating people unfairly. Read what John says to them. Is there a way you can begin treating people more fairly?

Rate the level of satisfaction you have over winning when you play fairly versus when you play unfairly.

- Read 2 Timothy 2:5.
- Discuss the statement, "It doesn't matter whether you win or lose, it's how you play the game."

Take Action:

1. *Parent:* Have a family game night and instruct the child to play unfairly during the first game. Then, play the same game until the child wins fairly. Discuss how the child feels about winning fairly versus unfairly.

2. Memorize the following:

- Luke 6:31: The Golden Rule
- "It doesn't matter whether I win or lose; it's how I play the game."

FAITH

 **faith - n. 1.** Trust and confidence in someone or something. *Our coach has lots of faith in our team.* **2.** Belief in God. **3.** A religion.

Luke 5:20
When Jesus saw their faith, he said, "Friend, your sins are forgiven."

Galatians 3:26
You are all sons of God through faith in Christ Jesus.

Ephesians 2:8–9
For it is by grace you have been saved, through faith—and this not from yourselves, it is the gift of God—not by works, so that no one can boast.

Ephesians 6:16 ♥
In addition to all this, take up the shield of faith, with which you can extinguish all the flaming arrows of the evil one.

Philemon 6
I pray that you may be active in sharing your faith, so that you will have a full understanding of every good thing we have in Christ.

Hebrews 11:1
Now faith is being sure of what we hope for and certain of what we do not see.

See also: Matthew 8:26; 17:20; Mark 11:22; Romans 1:12; 3:31; 10:17; 1 Corinthians 13:13 ♥ ; 1 Timothy 4:12; 2 Timothy 2:22; Titus 1:1–3; Hebrews 11; 1 Peter 1:8–9

 **Discussion:**
Read and discuss Hebrews 11:1.

In whom do Christians have faith? Read Galatians 3:26 and Ephesians 2:8–9.

In what other things do people put their faith?[1]

◆ Are any of these things eternal?

Why is faith important? Read Luke 5.20, Ephesians 2:8–9; Ephesians 6:16.

If your parents are Christians, does that automatically make you a Christian?

◆ Think about Galatians 3:26 in relation to the phrase "God has no grandchildren."

Challenge:
Read Hebrews 11 to learn about people in the Bible's "Hall of Faith."

 **Take Action:**
1. Do you have faith in Christ? If not, refer to the topic Salvation.

2. *Pictorial representation of Ephesians 6:16:*
Draw a picture of you holding a shield labeled faith. Then draw flaming arrows coming at the shield. Label each arrow with something that attacks your faith. Write the verse at the top or bottom of the picture.

3. Read Philemon 6. Pray about and discuss how you can be "active in sharing your faith." Reference: Ministry.

Related topic: Salvation

---

1. Other people, other gods, career, possessions. Reference: Idolatry.

FIGHTING

 **fight - n. 1.** A battle between animals, persons, or groups in which each side tries to hurt the other. **2.** A hard struggle to gain a goal. *The speaker invited us to join the fight against poverty.* **3. v.** To have an argument or quarrel.

Matthew 5:9 ☺
"Blessed are the peacemakers, for they will be called sons of God."

2 Corinthians 10:4
The weapons we fight with are not the weapons of the world. On the contrary, they have divine power to demolish strongholds.

Galatians 5:14–15
The entire law is summed up in a single command: *"Love your neighbor as yourself."* If you keep on biting and devouring each other, watch out or you will be destroyed by each other.

1 Timothy 6:12
Fight the good fight of the faith. Take hold of the eternal life to which you were called when you made your good confession in the presence of many witnesses.

James 3:18
Peacemakers who sow in peace raise a harvest of righteousness.

1 Peter 3:8
Finally, all of you, live in harmony with one another; be sympathetic, love as brothers, be compassionate and humble.

See also: Galatians 5:22 🍇 ; 2 Timothy 4:7

Discussion:

Instead of fighting, what are some ways to handle a situation? Read Matthew 5:9.

➤ Calm down before continuing the discussion.

➤ Pray for guidance in how to make peace.

➤ Call in an adult or other young person to mediate.

Read Galatians 5:14–15.

◆ Who else is your neighbor besides the literal meaning of the people living next door?[1]

◆ Who are your closest neighbors?[2]

◆ Do you treat your family better or worse than other people? How should you treat them?

Most of the time you fight when you are angry. However, there are also times you want to fight because you feel strongly about something and the other person's opinion differs. Sometimes, in these cases, you may have to respectfully agree to disagree to resolve the fight. See 1 Peter 3:8.

What does 1 Timothy 6:12 say you should fight?

◆ What do you think 2 Corinthians 10:4 means?

◆ How can this verse be related to real life?

Take Action:

Is there someone with whom you frequently fight? Friend? Sibling? Parent? Make it your goal to try the methods listed under the first discussion question.

Parenting Tip:

Try not to fight with your spouse in front of your child. Disagreeing is fine, but fighting breeds insecurity and instability in the child's image of the family.

1. Classmates, friends, teammates, family.
2. Your family.

FORGIVENESS

> **forgive - v.** To pardon someone, or to stop blaming the person for something.

Genesis 50:17

"'This is what you are to say to Joseph: I ask you to forgive your brothers the sins and the wrongs they committed in treating you so badly.' Now please forgive the sins of the servants of the God of your father." When their message came to him, Joseph wept.

Luke 17:3

"So watch yourselves. If your brother sins, rebuke him, and if he repents, forgive him."

Luke 23:34a

Jesus said, "Father, forgive them, for they do not know what they are doing."

Romans 6:23

For the wages of sin is death, but the gift of God is eternal life in Christ Jesus our Lord.

Colossians 3:13

Bear with each other and forgive whatever grievances you may have against one another. Forgive as the Lord forgave you.

I John 1:9

If we confess our sins, he is faithful and just and will forgive us our sins and purify us from all unrighteousness.

See also: Matthew 6:12, 14; Ephesians 1:7; 4:32

Discussion:
Why is it important for us to forgive others? See Colossians 3:13.

- Is forgiving others a hard or easy thing to do?
- Do you think it was easy or hard for Christ to die on the cross so our sins could be forgiven?[1]

Take Action:
1. Do you understand what it means to be forgiven of your sins? Read Romans 6:23 and 1 John 1:9 and reference the topic of Salvation. If you read the plan of salvation and realize that you are ready to accept Christ or rededicate your life to Him, pray the prayer that is included in that section or your own prayer. Share your decision with your parents and your church.

2. Is there anything for which you need to ask forgiveness from God or your friends or family? Do that right now. Read Genesis 50:17.

3. Is there anyone you need to forgive? Do that right now. Read Luke 17:3 and Colossians 3:13.

Parenting Tip:
When your child purposefully does something wrong, help him learn to ask for forgiveness. He should say something like, "I'm sorry for _____. I was wrong. Will you please forgive me?" Having the child state what he is sorry for and admit he was wrong will increase the chance that he will not do it again. Asking forgiveness humbles him and helps him realize the impact his action had on the other person.

Related topic: Salvation

---

1. Hard: He endured mocking, beating, and a painful death. Look up Matthew 27:32–50.

FRIENDSHIP

friend - n. Someone whom you enjoy being with and know well.

Proverbs 12:26
A righteous man is cautious in friendship, but the way of the wicked leads them astray.

Proverbs 17:17a
A friend loves at all times.

Proverbs 18:24 (KJV)
A man that hath friends must shew himself friendly: and there is a friend that sticketh closer than a brother.

Ecclesiastes 4:10
If one falls down, his friend can help him up. But pity the man who falls and has no one to help him up!

John 15:13–15
"Greater love has no one than this, that he lay down his life for his friends. You are my friends if you do what I command. I no longer call you servants, because a servant does not know his master's business. Instead, I have called you friends, for everything that I learned from my Father I have made known to you."

1 Corinthians 15:33
Do not be misled: *"Bad company corrupts good character."*

See also: Psalm 119:63; Proverbs 22:24–25; 27:6

 **Discussion:**
List some qualities a friend should have.

- Do your current friends have these qualities?
- Do they see the same qualities in you?
- Read Proverbs 17:17a; and Proverbs 18:24.

What does "Don't judge a book by its cover" mean in relation to people? Think of an example.

Read Proverbs 12:26 and 1 Corinthians 15:33.

- Why does the Bible give these warnings?
- Do you have any friends that are likely to corrupt you or lead you astray? Who? What should you do?

Did you know that Jesus can be your Friend? Read John 15:13–15.

 **Take Action:**
1. Write your best friend a special note thanking him for being your friend. Encourage and lift her up by listing the good qualities you see in her.

2. Think of someone you would like to know better and find ways to befriend her.

3. Be a friend to someone who is frequently left out. Set an example to others by overlooking the person's differences (and finding common ground) in order to show friendship. Read Ecclesiastes 4:10.

Parenting Tip:
Get to know your child's friends and their parents. Help guide your child to friends of good character; steer her away from the bad, because at some point, the friends may have more influence on your child than you do.

FUTURE

future - n. The time to come.

Psalm 139:16b
All the days ordained for me were written in your book before one of them came to be.

Proverbs 3:25
Have no fear of sudden disaster or of the ruin that overtakes the wicked.

Proverbs 19:21
Many are the plans in a man's heart, but it is the LORD's purpose that prevails.

Jeremiah 29:11
"For I know the plans I have for you," declares the LORD, "plans to prosper you and not to harm you, plans to give you hope and a future."

Matthew 6:34
"Therefore do not worry about tomorrow, for tomorrow will worry about itself. Each day has enough trouble of its own."

Romans 8:28
And we know that in all things God works for the good of those who love him, who have been called according to his purpose.

Ephesians 2:10
For we are God's workmanship, created in Christ Jesus to do good works, which God prepared in advance for us to do.

 **Discussion:**
What do you think your future holds?

◆ What is your purpose here on earth?
Read Ephesians 2:10 and look up Psalm 86:12.

◆ Are you ever fearful about your future?
Read Proverbs 3:25 and Matthew 6:34.

Who is in control of your future?

◆ Ultimately, God is in control. Read Psalm 139:16; Proverbs 19:21; Jeremiah 29:11; and Romans 8:28.

◆ However, you can significantly impact your future by making good choices and leading a godly life.

 **Take Action:**
Pray for your long-term future.

Personalize these ideas and add your own.

➤ Future school options and decisions

➤ Wisdom in dating and finding a spouse

➤ Protection and strength against temptations

➤ Career path

Parenting Tip:
Pray ahead for your child. Use some of the ideas from Take Action and add your own. Most importantly, pray specifically. For example, when praying for the future spouse, pray for his or her maturity, spiritual growth, purity, and timing in your son or daughter's life.

Make an exhaustive and specific list of ways you can pray for your child's future and pray at least one item a day. Remember, praying for your child is the best investment you can make in his future.

GENTLENESS

gentle - adj. 1. Not rough. **2.** Kind and sensitive.

Proverbs 15:1
A gentle answer turns away wrath, but a harsh word stirs up anger.

Galatians 5:22–23
But the fruit of the Spirit is love, joy, peace, patience, kindness, goodness, faithfulness, gentleness and self-control. Against such things there is no law.

Ephesians 4:2
Be completely humble and gentle; be patient, bearing with one another in love.

Philippians 4:5
Let your gentleness be evident to all. The Lord is near.

Colossians 3:12–14
Therefore, as God's chosen people, holy and dearly loved, clothe yourselves with compassion, kindness, humility, gentleness and patience. Bear with each other and forgive whatever grievances you may have against one another. Forgive as the Lord forgave you. And over all these virtues, put on love, which binds them all together in perfect unity.

See also: 1 Peter 3:3–4, 15–16

 **Discussion:**
Read Proverbs 15:1 and think of an example.

◆ Why does a gentle answer turn away wrath (anger)?

◆ Why does a harsh word stir up anger?

◆ Does it do any good to stir up anger?

Read Philippians 4:5.

◆ Is your gentleness evident to all?

 **Take Action:**
1. Memorize Proverbs 15:1. Write it on a note card or paper and post it in a place where you will frequently see it. Try to live by it.

2. Colossians 3:12–14 Mobile:
Supplies:

◆ wire coat hanger

◆ construction paper

◆ markers or crayons

◆ string, yarn, or curly ribbon

◆ hole punch

Directions:

Take seven days (or weeks) to study each of the topics mentioned in Colossians 3:12–14. As each topic is studied, cut out a shape that resembles a piece of clothing from the construction paper. Write the topic on the paper, punch a hole in the top, and hang the shape from the hanger.

GIVING

> **give - v. 1.** To hand something to another person. **2.** To supply. *The new lamp gave us more light.* **3.** To offer. *We gave thanks that the rain finally stopped.*

Matthew 6:2–4

"So when you give to the needy, do not announce it with trumpets, as the hypocrites do in the synagogues and on the streets, to be honored by men. I tell you the truth, they have received their reward in full. But when you give to the needy, do not let your left hand know what your right hand is doing, so that your giving may be in secret. Then your Father, who sees what is done in secret, will reward you."

Acts 20:35

"In everything I did, I showed you that by this kind of hard work we must help the weak, remembering the words the Lord Jesus himself said: *'It is more blessed to give than to receive.'*"

Romans 13:7

Give everyone what you owe him: If you owe taxes, pay taxes; if revenue, then revenue; if respect, then respect; if honor, then honor.

2 Corinthians 9:6–7

Remember this: Whoever sows sparingly will also reap sparingly, and whoever sows generously will also reap generously. Each man should give what he has decided in his heart to give, not reluctantly or under compulsion, for *God loves a cheerful giver.*

 **Discussion:**
What can you give besides presents?[1]

Discuss times when you have found that "It is more blessed to give than to receive." Read Acts 20:35b.

What attitude should you have when you give? See 2 Corinthians 9:6–7.

What do you think the first part of Matthew 6:2–4 means?[2]

God gave us the ultimate gift. What was it?[3]

◆ Why is that so important to us? Reference: Salvation.

◆ Because God has blessed us with all we have, we should give God some of our time each day by spending it with Him, reading His words, and praying.

 **Take Action:**
Pick one of the following or think of your own idea:

➤ Give some of your belongings to the needy.

➤ Collect food for a food pantry.

➤ Help an elderly person with household chores.

Parenting Tips:
Teach your child to set aside a certain amount of money each week to give to church and missions: the principle of tithing. For tithing references, see Genesis 14:20; 28:22; Leviticus 27:30; Deuteronomy 14:22–29; 1 Chronicles 29:14; Malachi 3:8–12.

---

1. Sympathy, love, time, money, support.
2. Do not brag or boast about what you give.
3. He gave us His Son for our salvation.

GODLINESS

 **godly - adj.** Devoted to God; devout.

Psalm 4:3

Know that the LORD has set apart the godly for himself; the LORD will hear when I call to him.

1 Timothy 4:7

Have nothing to do with godless myths and old wives' tales; rather, *train yourself to be godly.*

1 Timothy 4:8

For physical training is of some value, but godliness has value for all things, holding promise for both the present life and the life to come.

1 Timothy 6:11

But you, man of God, flee from all this, and pursue righteousness, godliness, faith, love, endurance and gentleness.

2 Peter 1:3

His divine power has given us everything we need for life and godliness through our knowledge of him who called us by his own glory and goodness.

2 Peter 1:5–7 ✛

For this very reason, make every effort to add to your faith goodness; and to goodness, knowledge; and to knowledge, self-control; and to self-control, perseverance; and to perseverance, godliness; and to godliness, brotherly kindness; to brotherly kindness, love.

See also: 1 Timothy 2:1–2; 6:6

 **Discussion:**
What does it mean to be a godly person?[1]

◆ Can you ever be just like God?[2]

◆ Who do you know that exemplifies godliness? Why?

◆ What are some areas in your life that are keeping you from godliness? See 1 Timothy 6:11.

Read 1 Timothy 4:8.

◆ Why does godliness have more value than physical training?

Read 1 Timothy 4:7.

◆ What are some ways you can "train yourself to be godly"? See Take Action.

Take Action:
Parent and child: One way to learn godliness is to spend more time with God. Set the pace for your child's personal quiet time. Find an age-appropriate devotional guide at the Christian bookstore or library and teach him how to spend time daily with God. Do this until he desires to do it on his own or you feel like he should take on the personal responsibility.

Set an example by letting him see you having your quiet time. Discuss what both of you are learning.

Some families like to have daily or weekly family devotional times in addition to their personal quiet times.

Older child: Reflect on your life and pick one problem area to improve during the coming weeks. Find verses that will help instruct and encourage you in that area. Meditate on the verses. Pray that God will help you. Write down your growth, struggles, and successes in a journal.

1. Christlike qualities, high moral standards, good character, close walk with the Lord.
2. No, we are human and will never be perfect like Him. However, we can strive to live in a godly way as opposed to a worldly way.

GOODNESS

 **good - adj. 1.** Well-behaved. *Cynthia is such a good girl.* **2.** Of high quality, as in *a good piece of furniture.* **3.** Kind or helpful, as in *good to animals.*

Psalm 31:19
How great is your goodness, which you have stored up for those who fear you, which you bestow in the sight of men on those who take refuge in you.

Proverbs 3:27
Do not withhold good from those who deserve it, when it is in your power to act.

Proverbs 11:27
He who seeks good finds goodwill, but evil comes to him who searches for it.

Romans 12:9b
Hate what is evil; cling to what is good.

Galatians 6:9
Let us not become weary in doing good, for at the proper time we will reap a harvest if we do not give up.

Titus 2:7a
In everything set them an example by doing what is good.

See also: Psalm 23:6; Galatians 5:22–25 🍇 ; 2 Peter 1:5–9 ➕

Discussion:
Aside from the normal challenges that life presents, would you like to have life as easy as possible?

- Is life easier when you are good or bad? Why?[1] Read Proverbs 11:27.

Do you ever get tired of being good all of the time?

- Most young people do. Often, being bad seems like the easier, more fun choice. Help your child learn to think past the moment and drive home the message from Galatians 6:9 that states the payoff for being good will always far outweigh that of being bad. Look for real-life situations that support this verse, and use them as springboards for dialogue that will reinforce Galatians 6:9.

Read Titus 2:7a.

- Who is watching your example?
- What good and bad do they see you doing?

Take Action:
Memorize Galatians 6:9 so that when you are struggling between good and bad, reassurance from God's Word will come to mind.

Parenting Tip:
Teach your child to learn from others' mistakes. Use friends' situations, TV or movie scenarios, and current news events as springboards for discussion of how better decisions and good behavior could have spared the people grief, problems, and negative consequences.

---

1. It is easier when you are good, because you are not being disciplined and reaping the consequences for the negative behavior.

GOSSIP

 **gossip - n. I.** A person who likes to talk about other people's personal business. **2.** Idle talk about other people's personal business.

Psalm 19:14
May the words of my mouth and the meditation of my heart be pleasing in your sight, O LORD, my Rock and my Redeemer.

Proverbs 11:13
A gossip betrays a confidence, but a trustworthy man keeps a secret.

Proverbs 17:9
He who covers over an offense promotes love, but whoever repeats the matter separates close friends.

Proverbs 21:23
He who guards his mouth and his tongue keeps himself from calamity.

Proverbs 26:20
Without wood a fire goes out; without gossip a quarrel dies down.

James 1:26
If anyone considers himself religious and yet does not keep a tight rein on his tongue, he deceives himself and his religion is worthless.

James 3:5
Likewise the tongue is a small part of the body, but it makes great boasts. Consider what a great forest is set on fire by a small spark.

See also: Proverbs 18:8; Luke 6:45; 1 Timothy 5:13; James 3:3–10

 **Discussion:**
What damage can gossip do?[1] Read Proverbs 11:13; 17:9; 21:23; and James 3:5.

What is the most recent thing you gossiped about?

♦ What should you consider before gossiping?
Stop and ask yourself these questions:

✔ Would I want this passed around about me?

✔ Would I be embarrassed if everyone knew I started passing around the information?

✔ How would I feel if the person found out I was gossiping about her?

✔ Would others wonder if I gossip about them?

♦ Think before you speak. Remember Proverbs 21:23.

♦ What "calamity" could have been caused?

Take Action:
Play "Telephone" to Exemplify Gossiping:

➤ Sit in a line with at least 5 people.

➤ Person 1 makes up a detailed story about someone and whispers it to person 2.

➤ Person 2 whispers it to person 3, and so forth. Have the person on the other end say out loud what he heard. If the game has worked correctly, his story should vary from the original.

➤ Discuss the following questions.

♦ How did the story change?

♦ Why did the story change?

♦ If person 1 knew the story to be absolutely true, would it then be all right to tell person 2?[2]

---

1. Ruin a person's reputation, separate close friends, cause people not to trust you ...
2. No, it is still gossip.

GREED

 **greed - n.** Extreme selfishness; wanting everything for oneself.
greedy - adj. If you are **greedy,** you want more of something than you need.

Ecclesiastes 5:10–11
Whoever loves money never has money enough; whoever loves wealth is never satisfied with his income. This too is meaningless. As goods increase, so do those who consume them. And what benefit are they to the owner except to feast his eyes on them?

Matthew 6:19–21
"*Do not store up for yourselves treasures on earth,* where moth and rust destroy, and where thieves break in and steal. But store up for yourselves treasures in heaven, where moth and rust do not destroy, and where thieves do not break in and steal. For where your treasure is, there your heart will be also."

Matthew 6:24
"No one can serve two masters. Either he will hate the one and love the other, or he will be devoted to the one and despise the other. You cannot serve both God and Money."

Mark 8:36
"What good is it for a man to gain the whole world, yet forfeit his soul?"

Luke 12:15
Then he said to them, "Watch out! *Be on your guard against all kinds of greed;* a man's life does not consist in the abundance of his possessions."

See also: Ephesians 5:3; Colossians 3:5; Hebrews 13:5; 1 Peter 5:2

Discussion:

Discuss the difference between the words *need* and *want*. Think of several examples for each.

- ◆ Which word, if taken to an extreme, becomes greed?

What are some things that bring out the greediness in you?

- ◆ Do any of those things have eternal value?
- ◆ Consider Matthew 6:19–21 and Luke 12:15.

Read and discuss Ecclesiastes 5:10–11. Do you know someone like this?

Read Matthew 6:24.

- ◆ Which master will you choose?

Take Action:

1. *Parent:* Take a tour throughout your home. Point out different objects and have the child label each as a want or a need.

2. *Parent:* One of the fastest ways to dispel greed is for a person to realize how blessed he already is. Involve your child in a ministry or community project that deals with underprivileged or critically ill children. Seeing the circumstances of others will help him gain perspective and have appreciation for what he already has instead of greed for what he wants. He will also grasp, in a very real way, the difference between the words *want* and *need*.

Parenting Tip:

Do not give your child everything he wants. Help him develop an understanding of the value of material items by encouraging him to save his own money for special wants.

Related topics: Contentment; Jealousy; Money

GUIDANCE

 **guidance - n. 1.** Advice or counsel, especially about a student's future plans, as in *career guidance.* **2.** Direction or supervision. *We learned to draw under the guidance of an expert teacher.*

Psalm 25:4–5
Show me your ways, O LORD, teach me your paths; guide me in your truth and teach me, for you are God my Savior, and my hope is in you all day long.

Proverbs 1:5
Let the wise listen and add to their learning, and let the discerning get guidance.

Proverbs 4:11
I guide you in the way of wisdom and lead you along straight paths.

Proverbs 6:20–22
My son, keep your father's commands and do not forsake your mother's teaching. Bind them upon your heart forever; fasten them around your neck. When you walk, they will guide you; when you sleep, they will watch over you; when you awake, they will speak to you.

2 Timothy 3:16–17
All Scripture is God-breathed and is useful for teaching, rebuking, correcting and training in righteousness, so that the man of God may be thoroughly equipped for every good work.

See also: 1 Chronicles 10:13–14; Psalm 5:8; Proverbs 11:14; 12:15

 **Discuss:**
To what or to whom should you look for guidance?

◆ The Lord (Read Psalm 25:4–5)

◆ Your parents (Read Proverbs 6:20–22)

◆ The Scripture (Read 2 Timothy 3:16–17)

Does anyone ever become so wise that they do not need guidance? Read Proverbs 1:5.

What happens when people don't seek the Lord for guidance?

 **Take Action:**
1. Write Psalm 25:4–5 on a note card and tape it to your bathroom mirror. Every morning as you are brushing your teeth, pray these words to God. Make it more personal by asking for guidance about the specifics of your day.

2. Follow 2 Timothy 3:16 and refer to the ultimate Guide book, the Bible, when you need guidance. Learn to use the concordance in the back of the Bible and topical reference books like this one to help you find verses to guide you in your problems. Then, take the verses to God in prayer and let Him speak to you concerning your specific situation.

GUILT

> **guilt - n. 1.** The fact of having committed a crime or done something wrong. **2.** A feeling of shame or remorse for having done something wrong or having failed to do something.

Psalm 32:5
Then I acknowledged my sin to you and did not cover up my iniquity. I said, *"I will confess my transgressions to the LORD"*— *and you forgave the guilt of my sin.*

Psalm 51:9–10
Hide your face from my sins and blot out all my iniquity. Create in me a pure heart, O God, and renew a steadfast spirit within me.

John 16:7–8
"But I tell you the truth: It is for your good that I am going away. Unless I go away, the Counselor will not come to you; but if I go, I will send him to you. When he comes, he will convict the world of guilt in regard to sin and righteousness and judgment."

Hebrews 10:22
Let us draw near to God with a sincere heart in full assurance of faith, having our hearts sprinkled to cleanse us from a guilty conscience and having our bodies washed with pure water.

1 John 1:8–9
If we claim to be without sin, we deceive ourselves and the truth is not in us. If we confess our sins, he is faithful and just and will forgive us our sins and purify us from all unrighteousness.

See also: 1 Chronicles 21:8; 2 Chronicles 33:23; Ezra 9:6; Psalms 103:12; 130:3–4; Proverbs 21:8; Ezekiel 33:10–11

Discussion:
Do you feel guilty about something you have done recently or in the past?

How does guilt make you feel?

Where does guilt come from and why do we have guilt?[1] Read what Jesus says in John 16:7–8. (In this passage the Holy Spirit is referred to as the Counselor.)

What should you do when you realize you are guilty of sin? Read Psalm 32:5; Psalm 51:9–10; and 1 John 1:8–9.

Once you ask forgiveness of your sins, what happens to your guilt? Read Hebrews 10:22 and Psalm 32:5.

Take Action:
Hebrews 10:22 and 1 John 1:9 Visual:
Hold ketchup and mustard over the kitchen sink and use them to write on your arm or hand the things for which you feel guilty. Pray and ask forgiveness for those sins. Then, literally wash them away. This, like baptism, symbolizes Jesus paying the price for your sins.

Related topics: Forgiveness; Salvation

---

1. The Holy Spirit alerts us of our sin through guilt so that we can know when we are out of line with God.

HABITS

 **habit - n.** Something that you do regularly, often without thinking about it. *Making my bed has become a habit.*

Psalm 19:13
Keep your servant also from willful sins; may they not rule over me.
Then will I be blameless, innocent of great transgression.

Matthew 26:41
"Watch and pray so that you will not fall into temptation. The spirit is willing, but the body is weak."

1 Corinthians 6:12b
I will not be mastered by anything.

2 Corinthians 10:4
The weapons we fight with are not the weapons of the world. On the contrary, they have divine power to demolish strongholds.

Ephesians 6:10–11 🛡
Finally, be strong in the Lord and in his mighty power. Put on the full armor of God so that you can take your stand against the devil's schemes.

Philippians 4:13
I can do everything through him who gives me strength.

Hebrews 4:15
For we do not have a high priest who is unable to sympathize with our weaknesses, but we have one who has been tempted in every way, just as we are—yet was without sin.

See also: Romans 6:14; Colossians 3:2; 1 Timothy 5:13; Hebrews 10:25

Discussion:
Make a list of your good and bad habits.

◆ How do your good habits benefit you?

◆ How are the bad habits not good for you?

Do any of the bad habits seem too hard to stop?

◆ Read what the Bible has to say about overcoming bad habits in 1 Corinthians 6:12b and Philippians 4:13.

◆ What do Matthew 26:41; 2 Corinthians 10:4; and Ephesians 6:10–11 tell you to do?

◆ Read Psalm 19:13, a sample prayer.

Do you think God understands your battle with bad habits? Why? Read Hebrews 4:15.

 **Take Action:**
Habit Transformation:
Can you turn bad habits into good? Sample chart:

Bad Habit	Transformation (Use Scripture to help.)	Good Habit
Regularly forget to make your bed	Find a way to remind and give yourself time to make the bed every day.	Daily make your bed.
Bite nails	Find a way to distract yourself when the urge comes—chew gum, paint nails, etc.	No nail biting (and nice-looking hands)

Related topics: Perseverance; Temptation

HATE

 **hate - v.** To dislike or detest someone or something.

Exodus 23:5
"If you see the donkey of someone who hates you fallen down under its load, do not leave it there; be sure you help him with it."

Psalm 97:10
Let those who love the LORD hate evil, for he guards the lives of his faithful ones and delivers them from the hand of the wicked.

Proverbs 6:16–19
There are six things the LORD hates, seven that are detestable to him: haughty eyes, a lying tongue, hands that shed innocent blood, a heart that devises wicked schemes, feet that are quick to rush into evil, a false witness who pours out lies and a man who stirs up dissension among brothers.

Proverbs 10:12
Hatred stirs up dissension, but love covers over all wrongs.

Proverbs 13:24
He who spares the rod hates his son, but he who loves him is careful to discipline him.

John 15:18
"If the world hates you, keep in mind that it hated me first."

Romans 12:9b
Hate what is evil; cling to what is good.

See also: Proverbs 25:21–22; Malachi 2:16; James 4:4

 **Discussion:**
What does God hate? Read Proverbs 6:16–19.

What should we hate? Read Psalm 97:10 and Romans 12:9b.

Explain that hate is a strong word and should never be used in reference to a person. God even instructs us to love our enemies (look up Luke 6:27–28). However, we can hate someone's actions and still love the person. Discuss this concept in relation to your unconditional love for him as your child. You may hate that he _____, but you still love him in spite of his actions.

- ◆ Who in your life are you tempted to hate?
- ◆ What is it that you hate about the person?
- ◆ Try to hate the person's actions without hating the person.

Are you hated by anyone? Read Exodus 23:5 and John 15:18.

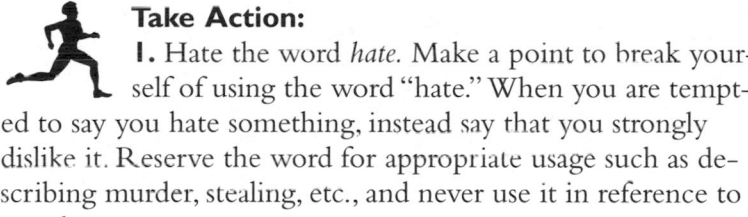 **Take Action:**
1. Hate the word *hate*. Make a point to break yourself of using the word "hate." When you are tempted to say you hate something, instead say that you strongly dislike it. Reserve the word for appropriate usage such as describing murder, stealing, etc., and never use it in reference to people.

2. Pray for the person today whose actions you hate and are tempted to hate as a person. If you have trouble with this, as most people do, ask for God's help. Acknowledge that while your hatred of his actions may be justified, you still need compassion for him as a person. Look up Proverbs 25:21–22.

HEALTH

 **health - n. 1.** Strength and fitness. **2.** The state or condition of your body. *Aunt Agnes is in poor health.*

Luke 2:52

And Jesus grew in wisdom and stature, and in favor with God and men.

1 Corinthians 6:19–20

Do you not know that your body is a temple of the Holy Spirit, who is in you, whom you have received from God? You are not your own; you were bought at a price. Therefore *honor God with your body.*

2 Corinthians 7:1

Since we have these promises, dear friends, let us purify ourselves from everything that contaminates body and spirit, perfecting holiness out of reverence for God.

3 John 2

Dear friend, I pray that you may enjoy good health and that all may go well with you, even as your soul is getting along well.

Drinking:
Proverbs 20:1; 23:20–21, 23:29–30; Romans 13:13; Galatians 5:19–25; Ephesians 5:18

Sexual Purity:
Genesis 2:23–24; 1 Corinthians 6:12–20; 7:9; 10:12–13; Galatians 5:16–26; Ephesians 5:1–3; Colossians 3:5; 1 Thessalonians 4:3–5

Smoking/Drugs:
Romans 12:1; 1 Corinthians 6:19–20; 1 Thessalonians 5:23–24; 1 Peter 5:8

Discussion:
Are you healthy? What are some ways to increase your health?

- ❖ Eat well-balanced meals.
- ❖ Eat in moderation.
- ❖ Never smoke or use drugs.
- ❖ Exercise.

Why should you strive to take care of your body?

- ◆ Read 1 Corinthians 6:19 20.
- ◆ What does it mean that "your body is a temple of the Holy Spirit?"[1]
- ◆ What does "you were bought with a price" mean?[2]
- ◆ How can you honor God with your body?[3]

Read the verses concerning drinking, sex, and drugs.

- ◆ Discuss the impact and ramifications of each on your health and the effect on those around you.
- ◆ Is indulging in any of these honestly worth the cost of disobeying God and putting your health at risk?

Take Action:
1. *Parent:* Make a health plan for your family. What does the family need to do to be more healthy? How can the family encourage each other?

2. *Parent:* Discuss potential problem situations (sex, drinking, smoking, and drug related) with your child and ask "What would you do if? . . ." questions to equip him to avoid trouble.

3. Encourage your church youth group to use the "True Love Waits" program, or something similar, which promotes sexual abstinence until marriage.

Related topics: Habits; Sickness; Temptation

1. If Christ is your Savior, the Holy Spirit lives inside you to help guide you (John 16:13).
2. Jesus paid the price for your sins by dying on the cross (1 Peter 2:24).
3. Eat healthfully; keep in shape; don't smoke; don't use drugs; don't have sex outside of marriage.

HONESTY

 **honest - adj.** An **honest** person is truthful and will not lie or steal or cheat anyone.

Exodus 20:16

"You shall not give false testimony against your neighbor."

Psalm 120:2

Save me, O LORD, from lying lips and from deceitful tongues.

Proverbs 12:19

Truthful lips endure forever, but a lying tongue lasts only a moment.

Proverbs 12:22

The LORD detests lying lips, but he delights in men who are truthful.

Matthew 5:37

"Simply let your 'Yes' be 'Yes,' and your 'No,' 'No'; anything beyond this comes from the evil one."

Luke 16:10

"Whoever can be trusted with very little can also be trusted with much, and whoever is dishonest with very little will also be dishonest with much."

I Corinthians 13:6

Love does not delight in evil but rejoices with the truth.

Ephesians 6:14

Stand firm then, with the belt of truth buckled around your waist, with the breastplate of righteousness in place.

Discussion:

Does lying sometimes seem like the easier route to take when trying to solve problems or get out of situations?

♦ In reality, why is lying not the easier route?[1]

Read the Bible verses and discuss what the Bible has to say about honesty, dishonesty, and lying.

Take Action:

1. Go to the library and find a collection of *Aesop's Fables* that includes "The Boy Who Cried Wolf." Read the story and interject questions throughout the reading. For example: After each time the boy cries wolf, ask what your child would do if he were a townsperson. At the end, ask if he feels sorry for the boy. Why or why not?

2. *Parents:* Work together on your family rules. Come up with levels of consequences that encourage honesty. For example, when a child does something wrong and lies about it, he will receive more consequences than if he told the truth. See first Parenting Tip.

Parenting Tips:

1. Always have consequences for wrong actions, but make them more extensive when the child does not tell the truth. This system will reinforce the importance of honesty and build a stronger trust between you and the child. *However, be careful not to minimize the wrongdoing by overly rewarding for honesty.*

2. Beware of "little" lies. For example, do not instruct your child to tell someone on the phone that you are not there. A lie is a lie.

---

1. Lies will always come back to bite you. One lie breeds another. People will learn not to trust you.

HOPE

> **hope - 1. v.** To wish for or expect something. **2. n.** A feeling of expectation or confidence. *I have plenty of hope for the future.*

Psalm 31:24
Be strong and take heart, all you who hope in the LORD.

Isaiah 40:31
But those who hope in the LORD will renew their strength. They will soar on wings like eagles; they will run and not grow weary, they will walk and not be faint.

Romans 4:18
Against all hope, Abraham in hope believed and so became the father of many nations, just as it had been said to him, "So shall your offspring be."

Romans 15:4
For everything that was written in the past was written to teach us, so that through endurance and the encouragement of the Scriptures we might have hope.

Romans 15:13
May the God of hope fill you with all joy and peace as you trust in him, so that you may overflow with hope by the power of the Holy Spirit.

Titus 1:2
A faith and knowledge resting on the hope of eternal life, which God, who does not lie, promised before the beginning of time.

See also: Psalm 130:7; Romans 8:24–25; 12:12; 1 Corinthians 13:13; 1 Timothy 6:17; Hebrews 6:18–19; 11:1; 1 Peter 1:3

 **Discussion:**
Have you ever hoped to do or receive something?

◆ Has everything you ever hoped for come true?

◆ Does that mean you should not hope for things?[1]

Do you sometimes feel like there is no hope? Read and discuss Psalm 31:24; Isaiah 40:31; Romans 4:18; and Romans 15:13.

Of what does God give us hope? Read Titus 1:2.

What tool has God provided for us to help give us hope? Read Romans 15:4.

 **Take Action:**
Hope Game:

Child Says ...	Parent Says ...
"I hope I will make the soccer team."	"I hope you do too, but either way we can be strong and take heart because we hope in the Lord." (Psalm 31:24)
"I hope I don't get sick over the holidays."	"Me too, but either way we can be strong and take heart because we hope in the Lord." (Psalm 31:24)

Once the child catches on, reverse the game and let the child encourage the parent. The repetition will reinforce and apply the meaning of the verse to the child's life.

---

1. No. It is good to hope for things in our daily lives, but the focus should be placed on spiritual hope since it is the only certainty. For application, see Take Action.

HOSPITALITY

 **hospitality - n.** A generous and friendly way of treating people, especially guests, so that they feel comfortable and at home.

Luke 6:27–28
"But I tell you who hear me: Love your enemies, do good to those who hate you, bless those who curse you, pray for those who mistreat you."

Romans 12:13
Share with God's people who are in need. Practice hospitality.

Titus 1:8
Rather he must be hospitable, one who loves what is good, who is self-controlled, upright, holy and disciplined.

Hebrews 13:2
Do not forget to entertain strangers, for by so doing some people have entertained angels without knowing it.

1 Peter 4:9
Offer hospitality to one another without grumbling.

Discussion:
What are some ways to practice hospitality?[1]
Read Romans 12:13.

Before you leave someone's house or party, what is the hospitable thing to do?[2]

Sometimes being hospitable puts you out. For example: Your grandparents come to visit for two weeks and will be staying in your room. How should you react to these kinds of situations? See 1 Peter 4:9.

Do you know anyone who is not very nice?

- ◆ Is it difficult for you to be hospitable to this person?
- ◆ Should you be hospitable to people even when they are not nice?[3] Read Luke 6:27–28.

Take Action:
Invite a friend over and practice your hospitality. Make a list ahead of time of ways you can be hospitable. For example: Let the friend pick what to eat and what games to play, let him go first, thank him for coming . . .

When the friend leaves, discuss the following:

- ➤ How did your hospitality make the guest's visit more enjoyable?
- ➤ Did you enjoy being hospitable? Why?

---

1. Common courtesies:"Please," "Thank you," open doors, pull out chairs, let guests go first . . .
2. Thank the host or hostess for having you over. Try also to thank him or her for specific reasons that made your time enjoyable.
3. At a minimum, you are always obligated to be polite.

HUMILITY

humble - adj. Modest and not proud.
humility - n. If you show **humility,** you are not too proud, and you recognize your own faults.

2 Chronicles 7:14

"If my people, who are called by my name, will humble themselves and pray and seek my face and turn from their wicked ways, then will I hear from heaven and will forgive their sin and will heal their land."

Proverbs 11:2

When pride comes, then comes disgrace, but with humility comes wisdom.

Matthew 23:12

"For whoever exalts himself will be humbled, and whoever humbles himself will be exalted."

Ephesians 4:2

Be completely humble and gentle; be patient, bearing with one another in love.

Philippians 2:3–4

Do nothing out of selfish ambition or vain conceit, but in humility consider others better than yourselves. *Each of you should look not only to your own interests, but also to the interests of others.*

1 Peter 5:5–6

Young men, in the same way be submissive to those who are older. All of you, clothe yourselves with humility toward one another, because, "God opposes the proud but gives grace to the humble." Humble yourselves, therefore, under God's mighty hand, that he may lift you up in due time.

See also: Matthew 18:4; 2 Corinthians 3:5

Discussion:
In what areas of your life do you need to work on being more humble?

What does Philippians 2:3–4 say we can do to learn humility?

Read Proverbs 11:2 and then read the definition of humble. How does the definition shed light on the meaning of the verse?[1]

Read Matthew 23:12. Can you think of anyone in your life or anyone famous who fits each part of the verse?[2]

Take Action:
1. Focus this week on not bragging about yourself or being conceited. Look for ways to lift up others through your words and actions. For example, if you make a goal at your soccer game this week, give credit to your team who helped you instead of taking all of the credit for yourself.

2. Practice 2 Chronicles 7:14. Humble yourself daily before God by seeking Him, confessing your sins, and turning from the bad things you are doing.

Parenting Tip:
Confessing sin is an important facet of prayer that is often overlooked. Teaching your child to think back through the day and confess his sins will not only help him be humble, but will also reinforce accountability for his negative behavior.

Related topics: Conceitedness; Pride

---

1. Not being aware of your faults can cause you to stumble over them and fall. By understanding your faults and working on them through the grace of God, you gain wisdom.
2. Hitler: part 1 of the verse; Jesus: part 2 of the verse

IDOLATRY

> **idol - n. 1.** An image or statue worshiped as a god. **2.** Someone whom people love and admire, as in a pop idol.

Exodus 20:3
"You shall have no other gods before me."

Exodus 20:4
"You shall not make for yourself an idol in the form of anything in heaven above or on the earth beneath or in the waters below. You shall not bow down to them or worship them; for I, the LORD your God, am a jealous God, punishing the children for the sin of the fathers to the third and fourth generation of those who hate me, but showing love to a thousand generations of those who love me and keep my commandments."

Ezekiel 23:49
"You will suffer the penalty for your lewdness and bear the consequences of your sins of idolatry. Then you will know that I am the Sovereign LORD."

Habakkuk 2:18
"Of what value is an idol, since a man has carved it? Or an image that teaches lies? For he who makes it trusts in his own creation; he makes idols that cannot speak."

1 Corinthians 8:4b
We know that an idol is nothing at all in the world and that there is no God but one.

1 Corinthians 10:14
Therefore, my dear friends, flee from idolatry.

 **Discussion:**
What are some things people put in front of God?[1]

◆ Could these things be considered idols?

What are your idols?

Can your idols ever be equal to God? Why not? Read Habbakuk 2:18 and 1 Corinthians 8:4b.

What does God command concerning idols? Read Exodus 20:3 and Exodus 20:4.

How are you instructed to deal with idols? Read 1 Corinthians 10:14.

 **Take Action:**
Make an honest list of what matters most to you; your priorities. Consider:

➤ what you love,

➤ what you spend the most time doing,

➤ who you spend the most time with, etc.

What can you do to make sure you are not putting anything on your list before God? Reference the parenting tip as it also applies to the child.

Parenting Tip:
Are you too busy or hurried to make time for God each day? Consider that even positive things can become idols if they push God out of your day. Make a conscious effort to put God *first* in the day and the rest will fall into place. You, your child, and others around you should notice the difference this makes in your life.

---

1. Money, sports, possessions, family, friends, school, job, boyfriend, girlfriend ...

INTEGRITY

 **integrity - n.** If someone has **integrity,** the person is honest and sticks to his or her principles.

1 Chronicles 29:17
"I know, my God, that you test the heart and are pleased with integrity."

Nehemiah 7:2
I put in charge of Jerusalem my brother Hanani, along with Hananiah, the commander of the citadel, because he was a man of integrity and feared God more than most men do.

Proverbs 10:9
The man of integrity walks securely, but he who takes crooked paths will be found out.

Matthew 5:37
"Simply let your 'Yes' be 'Yes,' and your 'No,' 'No'; anything beyond this comes from the evil one."

Mark 12:14a
They came to him and said, "Teacher, we know you are a man of integrity. You aren't swayed by men, because you pay no attention to who they are; but you teach the way of God in accordance with the truth."

Titus 2:7–8
In everything set them an example by doing what is good. In your teaching show integrity, seriousness and soundness of speech that cannot be condemned, so that those who oppose you may be ashamed because they have nothing bad to say about us.

See also: Psalm 15:4b

Discussion:

Talk about the definition of integrity in relation to people you know in order to help solidify the concept.

Think of a time when you or a friend were dishonest and then were found out. Read and discuss Proverbs 10:9.

Do you think other people notice your integrity? Read Nehemiah 7:2; Mark 12:14a; and Titus 2:7–8.

Can people trust what you say? Read Matthew 5:37.

Why is it important for people to trust you?

How does God feel about people of integrity? See 1 Chronicles 29:17.

Take Action:

Younger child: Refer to the topic Honesty, as it is closely related to integrity and is a less abstract concept.

Older child: People do not often praise others for qualities such as integrity, important as it is. Think back to the first discussion question. Who did you discuss that has integrity? Make it a point to let them know that you admire this quality in them.

Related topic: Honesty

JEALOUSY

 **jealous - adj.** If you are **jealous** of someone, you want what he or she has.

Exodus 20:17
"You shall not covet your neighbor's house. *You shall not covet* your neighbor's wife, or his manservant or maidservant, his ox or donkey, or *anything that belongs to your neighbor.*"

Proverbs 14:30
A heart at peace gives life to the body, but envy rots the bones.

Romans 12:15a
Rejoice with those who rejoice.

1 Corinthians 3:3
You are still worldly. For since there is jealousy and quarreling among you, are you not worldly? Are you not acting like mere men?

1 Corinthians 10:21–22
You cannot drink the cup of the Lord and the cup of demons too; you cannot have a part in both the Lord's table and the table of demons. Are we trying to arouse the Lord's jealousy? Are we stronger than he?

2 Corinthians 12:20
For I am afraid that when I come I may not find you as I want you to be, and you may not find me as you want me to be. I fear that there may be quarreling, jealousy, outbursts of anger, factions, slander, gossip, arrogance and disorder.

See also: Romans 13:9; Galatians 5:19–21, 5:26

 **Discussion:**
Think of things that your friends have that you don't.

- What are you jealous of?
- Would those things really make your life better?
- Do you really need those things?
- Read Exodus 20:17 and Proverbs 14:30.

What are some things that you have that others don't?

- Do you think there are people who would be jealous of what you have?

Point out that some people do not even have enough food to eat or a place to live. The last thing on their minds is the newest toy craze or clothing fad.

Have you ever been jealous because someone received an award, honor, or present that you wanted or thought you deserved?

- Instead of acting jealous, how does Romans 12:15a say you should act?

Take Action:
1. Personalize Exodus 20:17 and Romans 12:15a. Make these verses personal by paraphrasing. For example, "I will not be jealous of my sister's bicycle, my friend's toy, etc., but I will try to rejoice with people as I would hope they would rejoice with me when I am rejoicing."

2. Squelch the jealousy factor by realizing just how much you have for which to be thankful.

Related topics: Contentment; Thankfulness

JOKING

joke - v. To say funny things or play tricks on people in order to make them laugh.

Psalm 19:14
May the words of my mouth and the meditation of my heart be pleasing in your sight, O LORD, my Rock and my Redeemer.

Proverbs 8:13
To fear the LORD is to hate evil; I hate pride and arrogance, evil behavior and perverse speech.

Proverbs 11:17
A kind man benefits himself, but a cruel man brings trouble on himself.

Luke 6:31
"Do to others as you would have them do to you."

Ephesians 5:4
Nor should there be obscenity, foolish talk or coarse joking, which are out of place, but rather thanksgiving.

Colossians 3:8
But now you must rid yourselves of all such things as these: anger, rage, malice, slander, and filthy language from your lips.

Colossians 3:17
And whatever you do, whether in word or deed, do it all in the name of the Lord Jesus, giving thanks to God the Father through him.

See also: Luke 6:45

Discussion:
What are some things you can do when someone begins talking or joking about things they shouldn't? (change the subject . . .)? Discuss what these verses say about this issue: Proverbs 8:13; Ephesians 5:4; Colossians 3:8; and Colossians 3:17.

What are some questions you should ask yourself before playing a joke or a prank?

- Could this physically hurt anyone or anything?
- Could this hurt someone's feelings or upset someone?
- Would I *not* want this joke or prank played on me?

If you answered yes to any of the questions, you should not participate in it and should discourage the others involved.

What do Proverbs 11:17; Luke 6:31; and Colossians 3:17 say to you about your actions?

Take Action:
1. Go to the library and check out some joke books. Learn some hilarious clean jokes so that you will be prepared to divert the attention from the bad ones.

2. Prepare yourself. Think ahead: If the people you are with are wanting to play a bad prank, what are some ways you could handle the situation? (Encourage them to do something positive instead; get away from them; tell an adult.)

Parenting Tip:
Be careful about using sarcasm when joking with children. Young ones especially tend to take words very literally and may not grasp the intent of your meaning.

JOYFULNESS

joy - n. 1. A feeling of great happiness. **2.** A person or thing that brings great happiness to someone.

Psalm 16:11
You have made known to me the path of life; you will fill me with joy in your presence, with eternal pleasures at your right hand.

Psalm 68:3
But may the righteous be glad and rejoice before God; may they be happy and joyful.

Proverbs 15:30
A cheerful look brings joy to the heart, and good news gives health to the bones.

Romans 12:12
Be joyful in hope, patient in affliction, faithful in prayer.

1 Thessalonians 5:16
Be joyful always; pray continually; give thanks in all circumstances, for this is God's will for you in Christ Jesus.

Hebrews 13:17
Obey your leaders and submit to their authority. They keep watch over you as men who must give an account. Obey them so that their work will be a joy, not a burden, for that would be of no advantage to you.

See also: Psalms 19:8; 33:1; 66:1–2; John 15:10–11; Galatians 5:22–25 ; James 1:2–4

 **Discussion:**
What brings you joy?

When does 1 Thessalonians 5:16 say you should be joyful?

- ◆ Think of a recent situation that was hard for you.
- ◆ Talk about how you were able or could have found joy in that hard time. Look up and read James 1:2–4.
- ◆ Is it easy to have joy in the good times?
- ◆ Is it easy to have joy in the bad times?
- ◆ Is joy necessary in both? Why?

Does the Lord bring you joy? Read Psalm 16:11 and Psalm 68:3.

What is the easiest way to bring joy to others? Read Proverbs 15:30.

How can you bring joy to your parents and teachers? Read Hebrews 13:17.

Take Action:
1. *Parent:* Have your child write 1 Thessalonians 5:16 on a piece of paper, decorate it, and put it on your refrigerator. When someone in the family is feeling down, use this verse to help him find something for which to be joyful and thankful.

2. This week, practice smiling more frequently. Doing so will bring untold joy into the lives of others. See Proverbs 15:30.

3. "Sing joyfully to the LORD" (Psalm 33:1a).

Related topic: Cheerfulness

JUDGMENT

 **judge - v.** To form an opinion about something or someone.
judgment - n. 1. An opinion of something or someone. **2.** The ability to decide or form opinions wisely.

Judge/Judgment
Proverbs 3:21–24

My son, preserve sound judgment and discernment, do not let them out of your sight; they will be life for you, an ornament to grace your neck. Then you will go on your way in safety, and your foot will not stumble; when you lie down, you will not be afraid; when you lie down, your sleep will be sweet.

2 Corinthians 5:10

For we must all appear before the judgment seat of Christ, that each one may receive what is due him for the things done while in the body, whether good or bad.

Judgmental Attitudes
Matthew 7:1–5

"Do not judge, or you too will be judged. For in the same way you judge others, you will be judged, and with the measure you use, it will be measured to you. Why do you look at the speck of sawdust in your brother's eye and pay no attention to the plank in your own eye? How can you say to your brother, 'Let me take the speck out of your eye,' when all the time there is a plank in your own eye? You hypocrite, first take the plank out of your own eye, and then you will see clearly to remove the speck from your brother's eye."

See also:

Judgment: Proverbs 10:13; 14:15; 1 Corinthians 4:2–5
Judgmental Attitudes: John 8:7; Romans 2:1–4; James 4:11–12

Discussion:
Read the definition of judge and judgment and read Proverbs 3:21–24.

- ◆ How can good judgment help keep you safe?
- ◆ How does good judgment keep you from stumbling?
- ◆ Think about and discuss why good judgment will cause you to have sweet sleep.[1]

Read 2 Corinthians 5:10.

- ◆ How do you feel about appearing before the judgment seat of Christ? Reference. Salvation.

What do you think it means to be judgmental?

- ◆ Read Matthew 7:1–5.
- ◆ **Important:** The act of judging is sorely misunderstood. We often hear, "It's not Christlike to judge." That is not a completely true statement. God calls us to discern right from wrong (Proverbs 3:21–24). However, we must be careful not to overstep into harboring judgmental attitudes (Matthew 7:1–5). In other words, we can judge actions as being right or wrong, but God judges people.

  For example:

  o Suzy stole some gum.

  o Suzy was wrong.

  o Suzy is a bad person. *Judgmental statement.*

Take Action:
Memorize portions of Matthew 7:1–5 and Proverbs 3:21–24.

Related topics: Criticism; Discernment

---

1. Because you will have no regrets and you will not have a guilty conscience.

KINDNESS

> **kind - adj.** Friendly, helpful, and generous.

Proverbs 11:16–17
A kindhearted woman gains respect, but ruthless men gain only wealth. A kind man benefits himself, but a cruel man brings trouble on himself.

Proverbs 12:25
An anxious heart weighs a man down, but a kind word cheers him up.

Proverbs 14:31
He who oppresses the poor shows contempt for their Maker, but whoever is kind to the needy honors God.

Luke 6:31
"Do to others as you would have them do to you."

1 Corinthians 13:4♥
Love is patient, love is kind. It does not envy, it does not boast, it is not proud.

Ephesians 4:32
Be kind and compassionate to one another, forgiving each other, just as in Christ God forgave you.

1 Thessalonians 5:15
Make sure that nobody pays back wrong for wrong, but always try to be kind to each other and to everyone else.

See also: Galatians 5:22–23 ; Colossians 3:12–14 ; 2 Peter 1:5–9 ⊕

 **Discussion:**
What can you do to show kindness to others?

Why does the Bible say it is important to be kind to others?
Read Proverbs 11:16–17; 14:31; and Luke 6:31.

Do you ever have rough days?

◆ Be aware of and be sensitive to when your friends and family members are having a bad day.

◆ What kind things can you say or do to cheer them up?[1] Read Proverbs 12:25 and Ephesians 4:32.

How should you try to treat people who have wronged you?
Read 1 Thessalonians 5:15.

Take Action:
Parent: Role-play scenarios where one person is having a bad day and the other person is kind in some way. This will help prepare the child to be kind to others in real situations.

Example	Kindness Shown
◆ Friend's dog ran away	◆ Help make and post "Lost Dog" signs
◆ Friend's grandmother died	◆ Listen, send a card, make a meal for the family
◆ Friend made a bad test grade	◆ Offer to study together
◆ It's your friend's birthday	◆ Do something special for him or her
◆ Friend's mom is not feeling well	◆ Ask how you can help

---

1. Compliment them and tell them why they are special to you, sympathize with them, help them look at the bright side, offer to pray with them or for them, ask what you can do to help ...

KNOWLEDGE

> **knowledge - n. 1.** The things that someone knows; information. **2.** Awareness or a clear idea.

Psalm 19:7–8
The law of the LORD is perfect, reviving the soul. The statutes of the LORD are trustworthy, making wise the simple. The precepts of the LORD are right, giving joy to the heart. The commands of the LORD are radiant, giving light to the eyes.

Psalm 119:66
Teach me knowledge and good judgment, for I believe in your commands.

Proverbs 8:10–11
Choose my instruction instead of silver, knowledge rather than choice gold, for wisdom is more precious than rubies, and nothing you desire can compare with her.

Proverbs 9:10
The fear of the LORD is the beginning of wisdom, and knowledge of the Holy One is understanding.

James 1:5
If any of you lacks wisdom, he should ask God, who gives generously to all without finding fault, and it will be given to him.

See also: Joshua 1:8; Romans 16:19; James 3:13; 2 Peter 1:5–9 ✚ ; 2 Peter 3:18

Discussion:
Discuss the following saying: "The more you know, the more you know you don't know."

◆ Why is this an important concept to remember and understand?

Read Proverbs 8:10–11. Why is knowledge better than gold?

Look up and read 2 Peter 1:5–9. Why does it say we need to add to our faith knowledge, among the other qualities listed?[1]

Read Psalm 19:7–8. What are some ways you can add to your spiritual knowledge?[2]

Take Action:
Parents: Daily increase your child's knowledge by setting the pace for his personal quiet time. Find an age-appropriate devotional book at the Christian bookstore and teach him how to spend time with God. Enjoy sharing his devotional time with him until he desires to do it on his own or you feel that he should take on the personal responsibility.

Set a good example for your child. Let him see you having your quiet time. Discuss what both of you are learning.

Some families like to do daily or weekly family devotional times in addition to their personal quiet times.

Related topics: Choices; Discernment

1. "For if you possess these qualities in increasing measure . . ."
2. Attend church, Sunday school, Bible study, have a personal devotional time including praying and reading the Bible.

LAZINESS

> **lazy - adj.** If you are **lazy,** you do not want to work or be active.

Proverbs 10:4–5
Lazy hands make a man poor, but diligent hands bring wealth. He who gathers crops in summer is a wise son, but he who sleeps during harvest is a disgraceful son.

Proverbs 20:13
Do not love sleep or you will grow poor; stay awake and you will have food to spare.

Ecclesiastes 10:18
If a man is lazy, the rafters sag; if his hands are idle, the house leaks.

1 Thessalonians 5:14
And we urge you, brothers, warn those who are idle, encourage the timid, help the weak, be patient with everyone.

2 Thessalonians 3:10–12
For even when we were with you, we gave you this rule: "If a man will not work, he shall not eat." We hear that some among you are idle. They are not busy; they are busybodies. Such people we command and urge in the Lord Jesus Christ to settle down and earn the bread they eat.

Hebrews 6:12
We do not want you to become lazy, but to imitate those who through faith and patience inherit what has been promised.

See also: Proverbs 6:6–11; 19:15; Romans 12:11; Ephesians 5:15–16; Titus 3:14

 **Discussion:**
What is the difference between relaxing and being lazy?

Imagine what would happen if ...

- your mom and dad were lazy?
- your teacher was lazy?
- firemen and people of other professions were lazy?
- you were lazy?

What are some areas in which you have been lazy?[1]

Why should you strive to not be lazy? Read and discuss the verses on the previous page.

Take Action:
Develop a system that will help keep you from being lazy. For example: Use relaxing as your reward for getting things done. The sooner you complete your tasks, the sooner you can relax with a sense of accomplishment.

Parenting Tip:
First Thessalonians 5:14 says to "warn those who are idle." If your child is lazy or idle when he should not be, take this verse to heart. Warn the child of the consequences of this behavior and help encourage him out of the laziness.

Related topic: Apathy

---

1. Homework, chores, practicing an instrument, quiet time ...

LISTENING

 **listen - v.** To pay attention so that you can hear something.

Proverbs 18:13
He who answers before listening—that is his folly and his shame.

Proverbs 19:27
Stop listening to instruction, my son, and you will stray from the words of knowledge.

Proverbs 25:12
Like an earring of gold or an ornament of fine gold is a wise man's rebuke to a listening ear.

Acts 16:14
One of those listening was a woman named Lydia, a dealer in purple cloth from the city of Thyatira, who was a worshiper of God. The Lord opened her heart to respond to Paul's message.

Acts 16:25
About midnight Paul and Silas were praying and singing hymns to God, and the other prisoners were listening to them.

2 Timothy 3:16
All Scripture is God-breathed and is useful for teaching, rebuking, correcting and training in righteousness.

James 1:19
My dear brothers, take note of this: *Everyone should be quick to listen, slow to speak* and slow to become angry.

See also: 1 Samuel 3:9; Luke 10:39

Discussion:

It has been said, "God gave us two ears and one mouth for a reason." What do you think the reason for this might be? Read Proverbs 18:13 and James 1:19.

Who is the most important person to listen to? How does God speak to us?[1] Read 2 Timothy 3:16.

What do Proverbs 19:27 and Proverbs 25:12 say we should listen to? Why?

Do you think that what you say could have an impact on those listening to you? Read and discuss Acts 16:14 and Acts 16:25. You never know who could be watching or listening to you.

Take Action:

1. *Active Listener*

Conversation Checklist:

- ✔ Can the person tell that I am interested in what he is saying by my body language?
- ✔ Am I paying more attention to what I'm going to say next than to what the person is saying?
- ✔ Am I balancing what I have to say with listening to what he has to say?

2. Practice listening to God by meditating and appling specific verses. Read 2 Timothy 3:16.

Parenting Tip:

Make your child feel important by listening attentively when he talks to you. Whenever possible, stop what you are doing so that you can make eye contact and focus on what the child is saying. This will help promote open communication and signal to your child that you value what he has to say.

---

1. Through the Bible, ministers, others' actions and words, songs, and to our hearts.

LONELINESS

 **lonely - adj.** If you are **lonely,** you are sad because you are by yourself.

Genesis 2:18
The LORD God said, "It is not good for the man to be alone. I will make a helper suitable for him."

Exodus 18:18
"You and these people who come to you will only wear yourselves out. The work is too heavy for you; you cannot handle it alone."

Psalm 25:16
Turn to me and be gracious to me, for I am lonely and afflicted.

Psalm 68:6
God sets the lonely in families, he leads forth the prisoners with singing; but the rebellious live in a sun-scorched land.

Proverbs 18:24 (KJV)
A man that hath friends must shew himself friendly: and there is a friend that sticketh closer than a brother.

Luke 5:16
But Jesus often withdrew to lonely places and prayed.

Hebrews 13:5b
"Never will I leave you; never will I forsake you."

 **Discussion:**
Are you ever lonely? Pray Psalm 25:16 and Hebrews 13:5b and remember that God is always with you.

God knows we do not like to be lonely. Read what God did for Adam in Genesis 2:18.

Does it bother you to be alone? Why?
It is healthy to spend some time alone regularly.
Read what Jesus did when He wanted time alone in Luke 5:16.

Will you ever be truly alone? Read Hebrews 13:5b.

Take Action:
1. Are you lonely? Try Proverbs 18:24.

◆ To make new friends, sometimes you have to first be a friend.

◆ One of the best ways to shake the lonesome blues is to do something nice or helpful for someone else.

◆ Call a friend.

2. *Loneliness Squelcher:*
Do you know anyone who is lonely? What can you do to help squelch his loneliness?

◆ Give him a call.

◆ Invite him over to play.

◆ Introduce him to some of your friends.

LOVE

 **love - v.** To like someone or something very much.

Luke 6:27–28
"But I tell you who hear me: Love your enemies, do good to those who hate you, bless those who curse you, pray for those who mistreat you."

1 Corinthians 13:4–8a ♥
Love is patient, love is kind. It does not envy, it does not boast, it is not proud. It is not rude, it is not self–seeking, it is not easily angered, it keeps no record of wrongs. Love does not delight in evil but rejoices with the truth. It always protects, always trusts, always hopes, always perseveres. Love never fails.

Galatians 5:14
The entire law is summed up in a single command: *"Love your neighbor as yourself."*

1 John 3:18
Dear children, let us not love with words or tongue but with actions and in truth.

1 John 4:16b
God is love.

1 John 4:19
We love because he first loved us.

1 John 5:3
This is love for God: to obey his commands. And his commands are not burdensome.

See also: Proverbs 10:12; John 3:16; Romans 8:38–39; 12:9–10; Galatians 5:22–23 🍇 ; Colossians 3:12–14 ⌒ ; 2 Peter 1:5–11 ✛ ; 1 John 4:11–12; 2 John 5–6

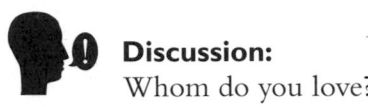 **Discussion:**
Whom do you love?

What are some characteristics of love? Read 1 Corinthians 13:4–8a.

How should you love others? Read Galatians 5:14 and 1 John 3:18.

Should you love only the people you like? Read Luke 6:27–28.

How can you love God? Read 1 John 5:3.

How does God love you? Read 1 John 4:16b and look up John 3:16.

Take Action:
The Gift of Love:
Parent: Help your child learn the Love Chapter, 1 Corinthians 13. Let her recite it as a gift to someone on a special occasion (i.e., her father on his birthday, the grandparents on their anniversary . . .).

Adaptation for younger children: Use the idea above, but choose only one of the verses or a smaller portion of the Love Chapter for the child to memorize. The child could also make a card with the verse(s) on it to give along with the recital of the verse(s).

MEANNESS

 **mean - adj.** Not kind, or not nice.

Psalm 71:4
Deliver me, O my God, from the hand of the wicked, from the grasp of evil and cruel men.

Proverbs 11:17
A kind man benefits himself, but a cruel man brings trouble on himself.

Matthew 5:44
"But I tell you: Love your enemies and pray for those who persecute you."

Luke 6:31
"Do to others as you would have them do to you."

Ephesians 4:31
Get rid of all bitterness, rage and anger, brawling and slander, along with every form of malice.

Discussion:
Read the definition of mean.

- Think about the way you act.
- Would anyone be likely to call you a mean person?
- Why or why not?

If you have any characteristics of meanness, what does Ephesians 4:31 say you should do?

Read Proverbs 11:17. How would being mean or cruel bring trouble on yourself?

How should you react when someone is mean to you?

- Is it all right for you to be mean back to someone who is being mean to you?
- Read Matthew 5:44 and Luke 6:31.

 **Take Action:**
1. Is someone being mean to you? Pray for him using Matthew 5:44, and pray for yourself using Psalm 71:4.

2. *Bury Your Meanness:*
Cut up slips of paper and write ways in which you have a habit of being mean on them. Dig a hole in the yard and bury the slips of paper. This will serve as a symbol of Ephesians 4:31 and a reminder that you have buried the meanness.

MERCY

 **mercy - n.** If you show **mercy** to someone, you do not treat or punish the person as severely as he or she may deserve.

Proverbs 28:13
He who conceals his sins does not prosper, but whoever confesses and renounces them finds mercy.

Micah 6:8
He has showed you, O man, what is good. And what does the LORD require of you? To act justly and to love mercy and to walk humbly with your God.

Micah 7:18
Who is a God like you, who pardons sin and forgives the transgression of the remnant of his inheritance? You do not stay angry forever but delight to show mercy.

Matthew 5:7 ☺
"Blessed are the merciful, for they will be shown mercy."

Luke 6:36
"Be merciful, just as your Father is merciful."

I Timothy 1:16
But for that very reason I was shown mercy so that in me, the worst of sinners, Christ Jesus might display his unlimited patience as an example for those who would believe on him and receive eternal life.

See also: Deuteronomy 4:31; Psalms 5:7; 6:9; Daniel 9:9; Hosea 6:6; Matthew 12:7; 23:23; James 3:17

Discussion:
Think of something you recently did wrong that got you in trouble with your parents.

- ◆ Could your parents have been harder on you than they were?
- ◆ Are they still holding the wrongdoing over your head?
- ◆ If not, then they have shown you mercy. Read Micah 7:18.

How does God show us mercy? Read Proverbs 28:13; Matthew 5:7; and 1 Timothy 1:16.

Challenge:

Does God's gift of grace and mercy mean that you can go on sinning whenever you want since you know He will be merciful? Look up and read Romans 6:1–4 and Romans 6:15–18.

Take Action:
1. Can you find a way to show mercy? For example:

- ◆ Let go of a grudge.
- ◆ Be kind to someone who has been mean to you.

2. Have you accepted God's grace and mercy?

- ◆ Reference: Salvation.
- ◆ Thank God for showing you His mercy.

MINISTRY

minister - v. To help or serve someone.

Matthew 25:40 (For the context, read verses 34–46.)
"The King will reply, *'I tell you the truth, whatever you did for one of the least of these brothers of mine, you did for me.'*"

Matthew 28:19–20
"Therefore go and make disciples of all nations, baptizing them in the name of the Father and of the Son and of the Holy Spirit, and teaching them to obey everything I have commanded you. And surely I am with you always, to the very end of the age."

Acts 8:21
"You have no part or share in this ministry, because your heart is not right before God."

Romans 10:15b
"How beautiful are the feet of those who bring good news!"

2 Corinthians 3:3
You show that you are a letter from Christ, the result of our ministry, written not with ink but with the Spirit of the living God, not on tablets of stone but on tablets of human hearts.

2 Corinthians 6:3
We put no stumbling block in anyone's path, so that our ministry will not be discredited.

See also: Matthew 5:14–16; 25:34–46; Mark 16:15; Romans 1:16a; Philemon 6

Discussion:
What are some different ways to minister to others? Look up and read Matthew 25:34–46 (verse 40 is listed).

Why should you minister to others? Read Matthew 25:40.

Ministering can also involve evangelizing (spreading the good news of salvation through Christ).

- ◆ Read Matthew 28:19–20 and Romans 10:15b.
- ◆ What impact can this type of ministry have? Read 2 Corinthians 3:3.

According to Acts 8:21, what is a qualification for Christian ministry?

Read 2 Corinthians 6:3.

- ◆ List some stumbling blocks.
- ◆ Discuss how a ministry could be discredited by these.

Take Action:
1. Call your church, find out what ministries children can help with, and make a commitment to get involved in one of them.

2. Make a list of ways to minister to others in your daily life.

3. Find a prayer guide for missionaries at your church or Christian bookstore. Make praying for missionaries a part of your daily quiet time. Look up and pray Ephesians 6:19 for them. Find where they live on a map and minister to them by writing them notes of encouragement.

Related topics: Charity; Giving; Talent

MONEY

 **money - n.** The coins and bills that people use to buy things.

Ecclesiastes 5:10
Whoever loves money never has money enough; whoever loves wealth is never satisfied with his income. This too is meaningless.

Matthew 6:24b
"You cannot serve both God and Money."

Luke 12:33
"Sell your possessions and give to the poor. Provide purses for yourselves that will not wear out, a treasure in heaven that will not be exhausted, where no thief comes near and no moth destroys."

Romans 13:8
Let no debt remain outstanding, except the continuing debt to love one another, for he who loves his fellowman has fulfilled the law.

1 Timothy 6:10
For the love of money is a root of all kinds of evil. Some people, eager for money, have wandered from the faith and pierced themselves with many griefs.

Hebrews 13:5
Keep your lives free from the love of money and be content with what you have, because God has said, "Never will I leave you; never will I forsake you."

See also: Psalm 49:16–20; Proverbs 13:11; Acts 2:45; 1 Timothy 6:17; 1 Peter 5:2

Discussion:
Can money buy happiness? Why or why not?

Can you be rich and not have a lot of money?
What are other kinds of riches?[1]

Read Ecclesiastes 5:10 and 1 Timothy 6:10.

- ◆ Discuss the meaning of these verses.

- ◆ Do you know people who fit the description?

What should your attitude toward money be? Read Luke 12:33 and Hebrews 13:5 and look up Psalm 49:16–20.

What is the word that describes owing money that you spent when you didn't really have it?

- ◆ What does Romans 13:8 say about debt?

 **Take Action:**
Parent: Decorate four jars or envelopes and label them as *Tithe, Savings, Missions,* and *Spending.* Decide how much of every dollar should go to each category. As the child receives money, he can put the proper amount in each place.

Older child: Let the child use the empty portion of an old checkbook register to help keep track of his savings.

 Parenting Tip:
Teach your child to be a wise spender:

- ◆ Let him make mistakes so he will learn lessons.
- ◆ Set a waiting period of three days if he really wants something in order to discourage impulse buying.

Related topics: Giving; Greed

1. Wealth in knowing Christ, wealth of love, wealth of family, wealth of friends, spiritual wealth.

OBEDIENCE

 **obey - v. 1.** To do what someone tells you to do. **2.** To carry out, or to follow, as in *to obey the law or to obey orders.*

Leviticus 25:18
"Follow my decrees and be careful to obey my laws, and you will live safely in the land."

Romans 16:19
Everyone has heard about your obedience, so I am full of joy over you; but I want you to be wise about what is good, and innocent about what is evil.

Ephesians 6:1–4
Children, obey your parents in the Lord, for this is right. "Honor your father and mother"—which is the first commandment with a promise— "that it may go well with you and that you may enjoy long life on the earth."

James 1:22–25
Do not merely listen to the word, and so deceive yourselves. Do what it says. Anyone who listens to the word but does not do what is says is like a man who looks at his face in a mirror and, after looking at himself, goes away and immediately forgets what he looks like. But the man who looks intently into the perfect law that gives freedom, and continues to do this, not forgetting what he has heard, but doing it—he will be blessed in what he does.

1 John 5:3
This is love for God: to obey his commands. And his commands are not burdensome.

See also: John 14:21; Colossians 3:20; 1 Thessalonians 4:7–8

 **Discussion:**
What rules do you have the most trouble obeying?

Why do you think those specific rules are in place?

Why do you think you need to obey the laws that God, the government, and your parents have laid out for you? Read Leviticus 25:18 and Ephesians 6:1–4.

 **Take Action:**
1. Review the family rules with your child or corporately write new ones. Let the child have input so he will feel ownership in the system.

2. Play a game the child is familiar with but drop all of the rules. The players can do whatever they want, whenever they want, and for whatever reason.

Discuss how the lack of rules equals chaos and that the rules are designed to make the game fun. Explain that it is the same when playing the game of life. God designed us, knows what is best for us, and gave us a rulebook—the Bible. It is in our best interest to obey and live by His plan.

3. This week, try extra hard to obey God, your parents, teachers, and other adults in every way. Do not complain or argue (Philippians 2:14), simply obey. At the end of the week, think about the following:

> ➤ Was life harder or easier this week? Why?
> ➤ Was life more peaceful this week? Why?
> ➤ Could you make it a habit to live obediently?

Related topics: Discipline; Goodness

PATIENCE

 **patient - adj.** If you are **patient,** you are good at putting up with problems and delays and don't get angry or upset.

Proverbs 14:29
A patient man has great understanding, but a quick-tempered man displays folly.

Romans 12:12
Be joyful in hope, patient in affliction, faithful in prayer.

1 Corinthians 13:4 ♥
Love is patient, love is kind. It does not envy, it does not boast, it is not proud.

Galatians 6:9
Let us not become weary in doing good, for at the proper time we will reap a harvest if we do not give up.

Ephesians 4:2
Be completely humble and gentle; *be patient,* bearing with one another in love.

1 Thessalonians 5:14b
Be patient with everyone.

2 Peter 3:9
The Lord is not slow in keeping his promise, as some understand slowness. He is patient with you, not wanting anyone to perish, but everyone to come to repentance.

See also: Galatians 5:22–25 ; Colossians 3:12 ; 1 Timothy 1:16

 **Discussion:**
What are some things that take patience?[1]

Read what the Bible has to say about patience.

Discuss how our society discourages patience in many ways. The attitude is: We do what we want, whenever we want, for whatever reason. We don't want to have to wait, even if it would be in our best interest.

- ♦ What are some examples and consequences of this impatient type of mentality?[2]
- ♦ Think about the link between impatience and the consequences of the actions you discussed. Is it worth it for you to be patient in order to avoid all of these problems? Read Galatians 6:9.

Take Action:
Parent: Help your child plant his own vegetable, flower, or herb garden from seeds. (Or, on a smaller scale, use a pot or window box.) Use the garden as an opportunity to relate to life what he is learning through the gardening process.

- ➤ Discuss and demonstrate how it takes patience and care to help the plants grow. Explain how this process relates to growing relationships between family and friends.
- ➤ Teach responsibility and the principle of harvest; you reap what you sow. Look up Galatians 6:7–8.
- ➤ Talk about how success and failure sometimes is and sometimes is not equal to the amount of work put into something.

1. Saving money for something you want, learning how to play an instrument or sport, dealing with a sibling that always seems to be bothering you ...
2. Impulsively spending allowance money = wished you had saved it for something better. Spending without having the money; i e., credit cards = debt. Premarital sex = unwed mothers, abortions, STDs, AIDS, emotional scars ...

PEER PRESSURE

> **peer - n.** An equal, or a person of the same age, rank, or standing as another, as in *a jury of one's peers.*
> **pressure - n.** Strong influence, force, or persuasion.

Exodus 23:2a
"Do not follow the crowd in doing wrong."

Proverbs 1:10
My son, if sinners entice you, do not give in to them.

Proverbs 4:14
Do not set foot on the path of the wicked or walk in the way of evil men.

Romans 12:2
Do not conform any longer to the pattern of this world, but be transformed by the renewing of your mind. Then you will be able to test and approve what God's will is—his good, pleasing and perfect will.

1 Corinthians 10:12
So, if you think you are standing firm, be careful that you don't fall!

Galatians 6:9
Brothers, if someone is caught in a sin, you who are spiritual should restore him gently. But watch yourself, or you also may be tempted.

See also: Esther 3:2; Psalm 1:1; Daniel 3; Galatians 6:1; Ephesians 5:6–17

Discussion:
Have your ever used the argument, "But everyone else is doing it?" Read Exodus 23:2a.

Think of some sinful things that your friends do that seem enticing to you. Read Proverbs 1:10 and refer to the topic Temptation for helpful verses dealing with not giving in.

Are there any areas of peer pressure that you think will not be a struggle for you? Read 1 Corinthians 10:12.

Read Proverbs 4:14.

- ◆ What are some of the consequences of not keeping your feet on God's path?
- ◆ What does God say about people who stay on His path? Look up Psalm 1:1.

Read Romans 12:2. List some ways you can "renew your mind" so that to know what God's will is and not conform to the world.

- ◆ Attend church, daily read the Bible, and pray.
- ◆ Surround yourself with Christian friends who will help hold you accountable.

Look up Daniel 3 and read how three men battled pressure and remained faithful to God.

Take Action:
Positive Peer Pressure:
Read Galatians 6:1 and discuss how peer pressure could be positive. The next time you are feeling pressured the wrong way, flip the situation, and try to be a positive influence on your friends.

Related topics: Conformity; Discernment; Temptation

PERFECTION

 **perfect - adj.** Without any flaws or mistakes, as in *a perfect apple* or *a perfect copy.*

Psalm 18:30–32
As for God, his way is perfect; the word of the LORD is flawless. He is a shield for all who take refuge in him. For who is God besides the LORD? And who is the Rock except our God? *It is God who arms me with strength and makes my way perfect.*

Psalm 19:7
The law of the LORD is perfect, reviving the soul. The statutes of the LORD are trustworthy, making wise the simple.

1 Corinthians 10:31
So whether you eat or drink or whatever you do, do it all for the glory of God.

2 Corinthians 12:9
But he said to me, "My grace is sufficient for you, for my power is made perfect in weakness." Therefore I will boast all the more gladly about my weaknesses, so that Christ's power may rest on me.

2 Corinthians 13:11
Finally, brothers, good-by. *Aim for perfection,* listen to my appeal, be of one mind, live in peace. And the God of love and peace will be with you.

Titus 2:7a
In everything set them an example by doing what is good.

See also: Hebrews 7:11–28

Discussion:
Who is the only one who is perfect? Read Psalm 18:30.

Are you a perfectionist? Read 2 Corinthians 13:11 and emphasize that no human, except Jesus, will ever be perfect, but we can "aim for perfection" and do our best.

Psalm 18:32 says, "God . . . makes my way perfect." How does He do this? Reference: Salvation.

Are you weak in an area in which you wish you were strong? Read 2 Corinthians 12:9.

Take Action:
Aim for Perfection:
Draw a dartboard and write "Jesus" in the center ring. Cut, tape, and label each arrow with an area in which you will try to aim for perfection.

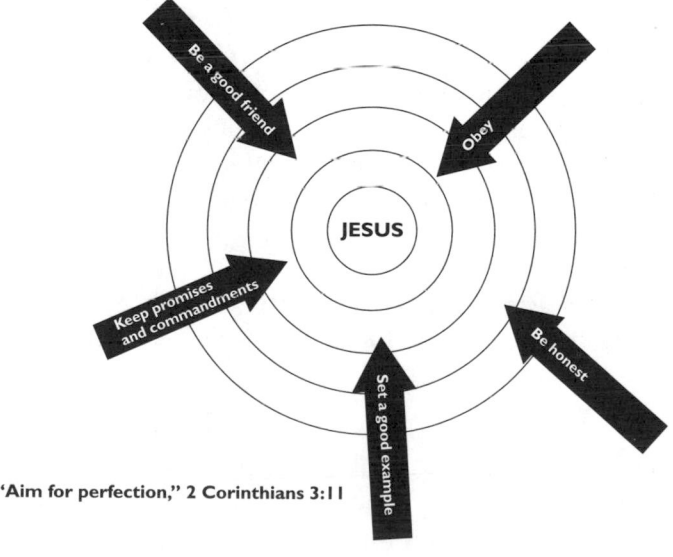

"Aim for perfection," 2 Corinthians 3:11

PERSEVERANCE

> **persevere - v.** If you **persevere** at something, you keep on trying and do not give up, even if you are faced with obstacles or difficulties.

Romans 5:2b–5

And we rejoice in the hope of the glory of God. Not only so, but we also rejoice in our sufferings, because we know that suffering produces perseverance; perseverance, character; and character, hope. And hope does not disappoint us, because God has poured out his love into our hearts by the Holy Spirit, whom he has given us.

Hebrews 12:1

Therefore, since we are surrounded by such a great cloud of witnesses, let us throw off everything that hinders and the sin that so easily entangles, and *let us run with perseverance the race marked out for us.*

James 1:2–4

Consider it pure joy, my brothers, whenever you face trials of many kinds, because you know that the testing of your faith develops perseverance. *Perseverance must finish its work so that you may be mature and complete, not lacking anything.*

James 1:12

Blessed is the man who perseveres under trial, because when he has stood the test, he will receive the crown of life that God has promised to those who love him.

James 5:11

We consider blessed those who have persevered. You have heard of Job's perseverance and have seen what the Lord finally brought about. The Lord is full of compassion and mercy.

See also: Hebrews 10:35–36; 2 Peter 1:5–9 ✚

 **Discussion:**
Read the definition. What are some things through which you have persevered? Are there people who go through life without having to persevere through difficult times?[1]

What are negative things some people turn to during difficult times?[2] Why is turning to God the most positive way to persevere through difficult times?[3]

Read Hebrews 12:1. God has "the race marked out for us." Learn to accept the trials that God gives you as His will. He will never give you more than you can handle. You may not always understand or know the reason why, but God has a bigger plan than we can see.

◆ What will be your reward for persevering? Read James 1:12 and 5:11.

Challenge:
Study Job (the book of Job) and Joseph (Genesis 37, 39–47) in the Bible. They are excellent examples of perseverance.

Take Action:
Perseverance Pays:

1. *Parent:* Ask the children's librarian to recommend an autobiography of someone who has persevered and overcome obstacles, such as a handicap.

2. *Parent:* To encourage perseverance in schoolwork, take your child to a workplace of his interest and discuss perseverance with the workers.

Related topics: Comfort; Hope; Suffering

1. No, trials are a part of everyone's life.
2. Running away from the problem, turning to drugs or alcohol, turning away from God, etc.
3. Because God is in control and the other ways are destructive and make matters worse.

PRAYER

 **pray - v.** To talk to God to give thanks or ask for help.

Luke 22:42
"Father, if you are willing, take this cup from me; yet not my will, but yours be done."

Romans 8:26–27
In the same way, the Spirit helps us in our weakness. We do not know what we ought to pray for, but the Spirit himself intercedes for us with groans that words cannot express. And he who searches our hearts knows the mind of the Spirit, because the Spirit intercedes for the saints in accordance with God's will.

Philippians 4:6–7
Do not be anxious about anything, but in everything, by prayer and petition, with thanksgiving, present your requests to God. And the peace of God, which transcend all understanding, will guard your hearts and your minds in Christ Jesus.

I Timothy 2:1
I urge, then, first of all, that requests, prayers, intercession and thanksgiving be made for everyone.

I John 5:14
This is the confidence we have in approaching God: that if we ask anything according to his will, he hears us.

See also: 2 Chronicles 7:14; Psalms 5:2–3; 50:15; Jeremiah 33:3; Matthew 6:9–13; 18:19–20; 21:13; Romans 12:12; Ephesians 6:18–19; Colossians 1:9–12; 4:2; Hebrews 4:16; James 5:16

Discussion:

◆ When can you pray?

◆ Does God always hear your prayers? Read 1 John 5:14.

◆ Does God always answer your prayers?[1] (Luke 22:42.)

◆ According to Philippians 4:6–7, what does prayer bring?

◆ What helps you when you do not know how to pray for something? Read Romans 8: 26–27.

Take Action:
1. *Parts of Prayer:*
Parent: Trace the child's hand on paper and cut out the pattern. Label each of the fingers with one of the parts of prayer. Use the hand as a visual reminder as you pray.

Praise: Thanking God for who He is.
Thanksgiving: Thanking God for what He has done.
Confession: Asking for forgiveness for your sins.
Petition: Asking God for help with things in your life.
Intercession: Asking God for help with things in other's lives.[2]

2. Keep a prayer list. Make a list of all the things you would like to remember for which to pray. When you tell someone you will pray for her, do not forget to put her on the list.

3. If you enjoy writing, try keeping a prayer journal. Writing will not only help you focus as you pray, but also give you a wonderful record of how God has worked in your life.

4. Memorize the Lord's Prayer (Matthew 6:9–13).

 Parenting Tip:
Pray Colossians 1:9–12 for your child.

1. Yes, but not always in the way you might expect or want. For example, in reference to Luke 22:42, Jesus still died, but was resurrected from the dead.
2. Adapted from "Five Kinds of Prayer," in *My Getting to Know Jesus Journal*, by Rob Sanders (Nashville: Broadman & Holman, 1999). All rights reserved. Used by permission.

PREJUDICE

> **prejudice - n. 1.** An opinion or a judgment formed unfairly or without knowing all the facts. **2.** A fixed, unreasonable, or unfair opinion about someone based on the person's race, religion, or other characteristic.

Acts 10:34–35

Then Peter began to speak: "I now realize how true it is that *God does not show favoritism but accepts men from every nation who fear him and do what is right.*"

Galatians 3:26–28

You are all sons of God through faith in Christ Jesus, for all of you who were baptized into Christ have clothed yourselves with Christ. There is neither Jew nor Greek, slave nor free, male nor female, for you are all one in Christ Jesus.

James 2:1–5, 8–9

My brothers, as believers in our glorious Lord Jesus Christ, *don't show favoritism.* Suppose a man comes into your meeting wearing a gold ring and fine clothes, and a poor man in shabby clothes also comes in. If you show special attention to the man wearing fine clothes and say, "Here's a good seat for you," but say to the poor man, "You stand there" or "Sit on the floor by my feet," have you not discriminated among yourselves and become judges with evil thoughts? Listen, my dear brothers: Has not God chosen those who are poor in the eyes of the world to be rich in faith and to inherit the kingdom he promised those who love him? . . . If you really keep the royal law found in Scripture, *"Love your neighbor as yourself,"* you are doing right. But if you show favoritism, you sin and are convicted by the law as lawbreakers.

See also: Leviticus 19:15; 1 Samuel 16:7; Esther 3:5–6

 **Discussion:**
Read the definitions of prejudice.

Using these definitions, is there anyone you dislike?

Does God show favoritism? Read Acts 10:34–35 and Galatians 3:26–28.

If God does not show favoritism, should you? Read James 2:1–5, 8–9.

Think about the example of the rich and poor man given in the James passage.

- ◆ Have you ever shown favoritism in a similar way?
- ◆ Have you ever been subjected to that kind of treatment?
- ◆ How did it make you feel?
- ◆ Imagine if everyone followed the command to "Love your neighbor as yourself." Would there be any prejudice or favoritism?

Take Action:
"Love your neighbor as yourself" and learn from him or her. When you are tempted to show favoritism or be prejudiced because of people's differences, take it as a challenge to get to know them and see what you can learn from them.

PRIDE

> **pride - n. 1.** Self-respect, or a sense of your own importance or worth. **2.** A feeling of satisfaction in something that you or someone else has achieved. **3.** A too-high opinion of your own importance and cleverness.

Proverbs 8:13
To fear the LORD is to hate evil; I hate pride and arrogance, evil behavior and perverse speech.

Proverbs 13:10
Pride only breeds quarrels, but wisdom is found in those who take advice.

Proverbs 16:18
Pride goes before destruction, a haughty spirit before a fall.

Romans 12:16b
Do not be proud, but be willing to associate with people of low position. Do not be conceited.

2 Corinthians 7:4
I have great confidence in you; I take great pride in you. I am greatly encouraged; in all our troubles my joy knows no bounds.

Galatians 6:4–5
Each one should test his own actions. Then he can take pride in himself, without comparing himself to somebody else, for each one should carry his own load.

See also: Chronicles 26:16; Proverbs 11:2; 16:5; Romans 12:3

Discussion:
There are two types of pride; good pride and bad pride.

Look at the definitions of pride and determine which definitions mean good pride and which mean bad pride. Discuss examples of each.

Read and discuss all the verses on the previous page and determine the kind of pride to which each Bible verse refers.

Take Action:
1. A good way to combat pride is to practice humility. Remember this week to lift up others instead of yourself.

2. Draw a T-chart like the one below. Make a list under the good pride column of the characteristics and abilities of which you are proud. Then list under the bad pride column how each good example could be turned negative.

Good Pride	Bad Pride
What are you proud of about yourself? Samples: ♦ a great ball player ♦ good friend to others	How could these things turn into bad pride? Samples: ♦ take all the credit when it's a team effort ♦ act like you are doing them a favor by being their friend

Related topics: Humility; Self-respect

PROCRASTINATION

procrastinate - v. To put off doing something that you have to do simply because you don't want to do it.

Psalm 119:60

I will hasten and not delay to obey your commands.

Matthew 24:44

"So you also must be ready, because the Son of Man will come at an hour when you do not expect him."

Luke 14:18–20

"But they all alike began to make excuses. The first said, 'I have just bought a field, and I must go and see it. Please excuse me.' Another said, 'I have just bought five yoke of oxen, and I'm on my way to try them out. Please excuse me.' Still another said, 'I just got married so I can't come.'"

Colossians 3:17

And whatever you do, whether in word or deed, do it all in the name of the Lord Jesus, giving thanks to God the Father through him.

 **Discussion:**
In what areas do you find yourself procrastinating?

What are some consequences of putting things off and leaving them to the last minute? For example, if you procrastinate about your schoolwork, you may run out of time and not get it done or may do a poor job because you rushed to finish.

Do you obey and do things immediately when you are told or do you procrastinate and/or make excuses to the point that someone has to ask you to do it again? Read Psalm 119:60 and Luke 14:18–20.

Have you been procrastinating about accepting Christ as your Savior? Read Matthew 24:44. Reference: Salvation.

Take Action:
Is there anything that you need to take care of that you have been putting off? Make an action plan to complete the task. Think of a small reward to help motivate you. Read Colossians 3:17.

The things people procrastinate about are usually the things they dread doing. Make a habit of doing these first. Often, you will find the job was not as bad or took as long as you thought it would and you will feel an inner satisfaction not having it hanging over your head. Also, you will not be put in a bind later on if something else comes up that you need to do or would rather do than completing what you procrastinated about.

Parenting Tip:
Take away privileges (i.e., watching TV, playing with friends) until things that were procrastinated have been done. Teach your child to make a habit of not putting things off.

Related topics: Apathy; Laziness

RESPECT

> **respect - 1. v.** To admire and have a high opinion of someone. **2. n.** A feeling of admiration or consideration for someone that makes you take the person seriously.

Leviticus 19:3
"*Each of you must respect his mother and father,* and you must observe my Sabbaths. I am the LORD your God."

Leviticus 19:32
"Rise in the presence of the aged, *show respect for the elderly and revere your God.* I am the LORD."

Proverbs 11:16a
A kindhearted woman gains respect.

1 Thessalonians 4:11–12a
Make it your ambition to lead a quiet life, to mind your own business and to work with your hands, just as we told you, so that your daily life may win the respect of outsiders.

1 Thessalonians 5:12b
Respect those who work hard among you, who are over you in the Lord and who admonish you.

Hebrews 13:17
Obey your leaders and submit to their authority. They keep watch over you as men who must give an account. Obey them so that their work will be a joy, not a burden, for that would be of no advantage to you.

1 Peter 2:17
Show proper respect to everyone: Love the brotherhood of believers, fear God, honor the king.

Discussion:
Who deserves your respect? Read Leviticus 19:3, 32;
1 Thessalonians 5:12; and 1 Peter 2:17.

What else deserves your respect?[1]

How do you earn the respect of others? Read Proverbs 11:16a
and 1 Thessalonians 4:11–12a.

Take Action:
Hunt for Disrespectfulness:
Your goal today, or for any set period of time, is to
find as many examples of disrespectfulness as possible. Look for
it at the store, on TV, at school, at home, or wherever you go.
Report each instance to your parent and discuss how the situation could have been handled respectfully.

Parenting Tip:
Your child's respect for your position as a parent is
closely linked to discipline. Never forget that you are the parent and he is the child! Do not try to be his buddy. It is infi-
nitely more important for your child to respect you than to
like you, although both are possible. He will quickly lose respect for you if he sees he has control over you.

Ways to Gain Respect and Teach Your Child to Respect You:

➤ Always follow through with immediate and appropriate consequences.

➤ Admit, apologize, and ask forgiveness when you make
mistakes.

➤ Make "Yes ma'am," "No sir," "Please," and "Thank
you" a must.

Related topic: Self-respect

1. Life, our property and that of others, nature, privacy, beliefs and rights of others ...

RESPONSIBILITY

 **responsible - adj. 1.** If someone is **responsible** for something, he or she has to do it, and it is the person's fault if it goes wrong. **2.** If a person is **responsible,** he or she is sensible and can be trusted.

Genesis 3:12
The man said, "The woman you put here with me—she gave me some fruit from the tree, and I ate it."

Matthew 25:23
"His master replied, 'Well done, good and faithful servant! You have been faithful with a few things; I will put you in charge of many things. Come and share your master's happiness!' "

Romans 14:12
So then, each of us will give an account of himself to God.

1 Corinthians 4:2
Now it is required that those who have been given a trust must prove faithful.

Hebrews 4:13
Nothing in all creation is hidden from God's sight. Everything is uncovered and laid bare before the eyes of him to whom we must give account.

See also: Genesis 1:26; 43:9; Jeremiah 31:29–30; Romans 12:6–8; Galatians 6:5; Titus 3:14

Discussion:
Who is responsible for your actions?

◆ In light of Romans 14:12, does it do any good to shift blame to others? For example, read Genesis 3:12.

Is it all right to do something wrong when nobody will ever know? Read Hebrews 4:13.

Have you ever said, "He *made* me do it!" or, "She *made* me mad!"?

◆ Can anyone truly make you do anything or feel a certain way?[1]

Are you responsible? Read Matthew 25:23 and 1 Corinthians 4:2.

Take Action:
Remember that you are responsible for your own actions. Make choices that will please God. Ask yourself, "What would Jesus do (WWJD)?"

Parenting Tip:
1. It is of utmost importance to teach your child that he is responsible for his own choices and that actions have consequences. Use the "Choice Method": When your child is about to do something wrong, put the ball in his court by telling him he can choose to do right or wrong. For example: Say, "You can choose to put that down and not get in trouble. Or, you can continue playing with it and have _____ happen to you as a consequence. It is your choice." This method teaches and encourages personal responsibility.

2. Pray that your child will get caught in wrongdoing so that he can be held responsible for his actions.

---

1. No. You are responsible for your words, actions, and reactions.

REVENGE

 **revenge – n.** Action that you take to pay someone back for harm that the person has done to you or to someone you care about.

Leviticus 19:18
"Do not seek revenge or bear a grudge against one of your people, but love your neighbor as yourself. I am the LORD."

Proverbs 20:22
Do not say, "I'll pay you back for this wrong!" Wait for the LORD, and he will deliver you.

Romans 12:17–21
Do not repay anyone evil for evil. Be careful to do what is right in the eyes of everybody. If it is possible, as far as it depends on you, live at peace with everyone. Do not take revenge, my friends, but leave room for God's wrath, for it is written: *"It is mine to avenge; I will repay," says the Lord.* On the contrary: "If your enemy is hungry, feed him; if he is thirsty, give him something to drink. In doing this, you will heap burning coals on his head." *Do not be overcome by evil, but overcome evil with good.*

1 Thessalonians 5:15
Make sure that nobody pays back wrong for wrong, but always try to be kind to each other and to everyone else.

2 Thessalonians 1:6
God is just: He will pay back trouble to those who trouble you.

1 Peter 3:9
Do not repay evil with evil or insult with insult, but with blessing, because to this you were called so that you may inherit a blessing.

See also: Deuteronomy 32:35; 1 Peter 2:21–23

Discussion:
Think of a time when someone was really mean to you or wronged you in some way.

♦ How did you react?

♦ Did you find yourself wanting to get back at the person? Read Leviticus 19:18; 1 Thessalonians 5:15; and 1 Peter 3:9.

After reading the last three verses, are you wondering why you should be kind to someone against whom you would rather get revenge?

♦ Read Romans 12:17–21 and pay attention to the last part of the passage.

♦ Think back to your response to the first discussion question. Imagine the two ways you could have reacted: with kindness or with revenge.

   o Which do you think would have made more of an impact on the person who wronged you? Why?

   o Which would leave you feeling better about yourself and in the right standing with God?

   o Read 2 Thessalonians 1:6. Wouldn't you rather always let God handle the person in the way He sees is best instead of taking revenge yourself?

Take Action:
Make "Overcome evil with good" your motto (Romans 12:21). When someone wrongs you, look for ways to surprise him with kindness. By reacting this way, you will be ministering to others when they least expect it and in a way that will certainly catch their attention.

REVERENCE

 **reverence - n.** Great respect and love. *Everyone expressed reverence for the retiring teacher.*

Exodus 3:5–6
"Do not come any closer," God said. "Take off your sandals, for the place where you are standing is holy ground." Then he said, "I am the God of your father, the God of Abraham, the God of Isaac and the God of Jacob." At this, Moses hid his face, because he was afraid to look at God.

Leviticus 19:30
"*Observe my Sabbaths and have reverence for my sanctuary.* I am the LORD."

Leviticus 19:32
"Rise in the presence of the aged, show respect for the elderly and revere your God. I am the LORD."

2 Corinthians 7:1
Since we have these promises, dear friends, let us purify ourselves from everything that contaminates body and spirit, perfecting holiness out of reverence for God.

Ephesians 5:21
Submit to one another out of reverence for Christ.

Hebrews 12:28–29
Therefore, since we are receiving a kingdom that cannot be shaken, let us be thankful, and so *worship God acceptably with reverence and awe*, for our "God is a consuming fire."

See also: 1 Chronicles 16:28–36

Discussion:
Read Leviticus 19:30. What are some things that show a lack of reverence for His sanctuary?

- Dressing immodestly to attend church.
- Writing in the hymnbooks or on the bathroom walls.
- Talking or passing notes during the service.

Read Hebrews 12:28–29. How can you "worship God acceptably with reverence and awe"?

- Confess your sins and try to live a holy life (see 2 Corinthians 7:1).
- Put others ahead of yourself (Ephesians 5:21).
- Spend time with Him daily and read His Word.
- Show reverence for His sanctuary (see above).

Take Action:
Reverence Builders.
Parent: During breakfast on Sunday, pray that God will prepare the hearts of the family for worship and learning. Give the child one of the following ideas to help him focus and pay attention during the service.

- Make a list of the Bible verses used during the service. Decide which one you like best and tell why.
- Count the number of times the minister says the word, "_____."
- Think about and make notes for why you think the sermon was given a particular title.
- Make a list of the things that the pastor says that you think are interesting.

On the way home from church or at lunch, make it a priority to discuss what each family member learned.

Related topic: Respect

SADNESS

 **sad - adj. 1.** Unhappy or sorrowful. **2.** Something that is **sad** makes you feel unhappy, as in *sad news* or *a sad sight.*

Psalm 31:9
Be merciful to me, O LORD, for I am in distress; my eyes grow weak with sorrow, my soul and my body with grief.

Psalm 119:28
My soul is weary with sorrow; strengthen me according to your word.

Ecclesiastes 3:1, 4
There is a time for everything, and a season for every activity under heaven: . . . a time to weep and a time to laugh, a time to mourn and a time to dance.

Jeremiah 31:13
"Then maidens will dance and be glad, young men and old as well. I will turn their mourning into gladness; I will give them comfort and joy instead of sorrow."

Matthew 5:4
"Blessed are those who mourn, for they will be comforted."

Matthew 11:28
"Come to me, all you who are weary and burdened, and I will give you rest."

Revelation 21:4
"He will wipe every tear from their eyes. There will be no more death or mourning or crying or pain, for the old order of things has passed away."

See also: 2 Corinthians 7:10

Discussion:
What has made you sad recently?

♦ Have you felt like the psalmist in Psalm 31:9?
♦ Did you know that the Lord cares about your sadness and wants to help? Read Psalm 119:28; Jeremiah 31:13; and Matthew 11:28.

Is it possible to go through life without sadness? Is it OK to be sad and cry? Read Ecclesiastes 3:1, 4.

Will there ever be a time when there will be no sadness?[1] Read Revelation 21:4.

Take Action:
1. Are you sad? Share with someone what is making you sad. Often, just talking about your feelings will make you feel better.

Sadness can also be handled by taking action with a related topic. Pick one or more of the related topics listed below to study to help you with your sadness. For example, Psalm 119:28 says "strengthen me according to your word." Use the Scriptures under the topics of Cheerfulness, Comfort, and Joyfulness to help strengthen you.

2. Do you want to help someone who is sad? Think of a time when you were sad. What would have cheered you up? Use that idea for your sad friend.

Related topics: Cheerfulness; Comfort; Joyfulness; Suffering

---

1. Yes, in heaven.

SALVATION

 **salvation - n. 1.** The state of being saved from sin, evil, harm, or destruction. **2.** Someone or something that saves or rescues.

John 3:16

"For God so loved the world that he gave his one and only Son, that whoever believes in him shall not perish but have eternal life.

John 10:10b

"I have come that they may have life, and have it to the full."

Romans 5:1b

We have peace with God through our Lord Jesus Christ.

Romans 10:13

For, "Everyone who calls on the name of the Lord will be saved."

Ephesians 2:8–9

For it is by grace you have been saved, through faith—and this not from yourselves, it is the gift of God—not by works, so that no one can boast.

1 John 5:12–13

He who has the Son has life; he who does not have the Son of God does not have life. I write these things to you who believe in the name of the Son of God so that you may know that you have eternal life.

See also: John 1:12; Romans 6:23; Revelation 3:20

 **Discussion**

Our Problem: Separation
Why do you need salvation?

Romans 3:23
For all have sinned and fall short of the glory of God.

Our Attempts
What are different ways people try to gain salvation?

Proverbs 14:12
There is a way that seems right to man, but in the end it leads to death.

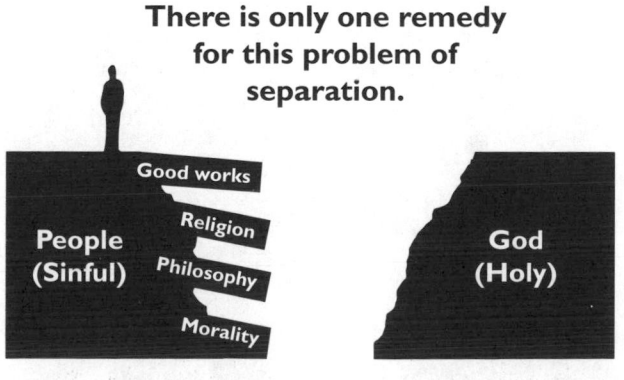

God's Remedy: The Cross
What has God provided for us to bridge the gap?

1 Timothy 2:5
For there is one God and one mediator between God and men, the man Christ Jesus.

See also: Romans 5:8; 1 Peter 3:18a

**God has provided the only way . . .
we must make the choice . . .**

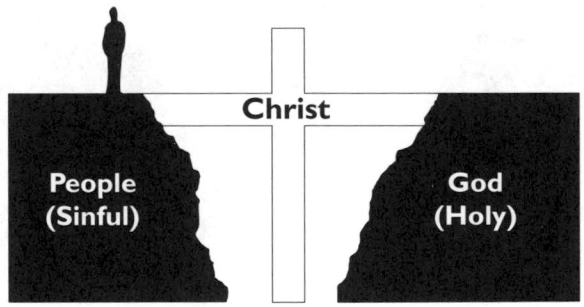

Our Response: Receive Christ
Do you trust in Christ for your salvation?

Romans 10:9
If you confess with your mouth, "Jesus is Lord," and believe in your heart that God raised him from the dead, you will be saved."

Are you here . . .   or here?

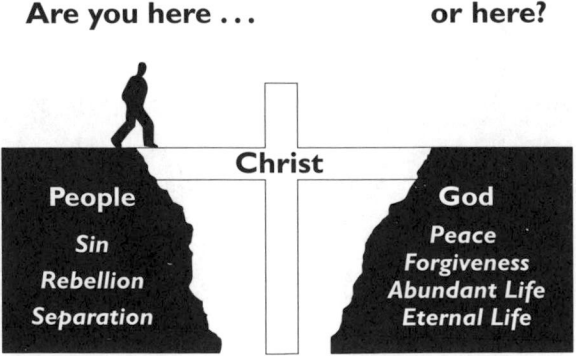

 **Take Action:**
How to Receive Christ:
1. Admit your need (I am a sinner).
2. Be willing to turn from your sins (repent).
3. Believe that Jesus Christ died for you on the cross and rose from the grave.
4. Through prayer, invite Jesus Christ to come in and control your life through the Holy Spirit (receive Him as Lord and Savior).

What to Pray:

Dear Lord Jesus,
I know that I am a sinner and need Your forgiveness. I believe that You died for my sins. I want to turn from my sins. I now invite You to come into my heart and life. I want to trust and follow You as Lord and Savior.
In Jesus' name, Amen.

What Now?

1. Be baptized as a public profession of your faith.
2. Pray and read your Bible daily to get to know Christ better.
3. Tell others about Christ.
4. Worship, fellowship, and serve with other Christians in a church where Christ is preached.
5. As Christ's representative in a needy world, demonstrate your new life by your love and concern for others.

The ABC's of Salvation:

Admit you are a sinner.
Believe Jesus is Lord.
Commit to follow Him.

SELF-CENTERED

 **self-centered - adj.** Thinking only about yourself; selfish.

Exodus 20:3
"You shall have no other gods before me."

Acts 20:35b
"It is more blessed to give than to receive."

Romans 12:10b
Honor one another above yourselves.

Galatians 6:3–5
If anyone thinks he is something when he is nothing, he deceives himself. Each one should test his own actions. Then he can take pride in himself, without comparing himself to somebody else, for each one should carry his own load.

Philippians 2:3–4
Do nothing out of selfish ambition or vain conceit, but in humility consider others better than yourselves. *Each of you should look not only to your own interests, but also to the interests of others.*

Discussion:
Read the definition and honestly consider whether others may perceive you as being this way.

◆ Do you think the whole world revolves around you?

◆ Do you expect everyone to always cater to your demands and wishes?

Do you like being around a person who only talks about himself and always has to have everything go his way?

What does the Bible have to say about self-centeredness?

Take Action:
Walk in Someone Else's Shoes:
Instead of thinking about yourself, put yourself in the shoes of those around you. For example: Instead of getting angry that dinner is not ready yet and complaining that you are starving, help your mother or father finish preparing the meal. He or she is probably as hungry as you are.

Parenting Tip:
If your child tends to be self-centered, involve her in activities that require her to look out for the interests of others.

Ideas:

◆ Match her with an elderly person in the neighborhood who needs regular help with household tasks.

◆ Require that she volunteer regularly at a local charity.

◆ Give her responsibilities related to the family pet.

Being responsible for the welfare of others will help your child take the focus off himself and give him a more balanced perspective on life.

Related topics: Conceitedness; Humility

SELF-CONTROL

 **self-control - n.** Control of your feelings and behavior.

Proverbs 25:16
If you find honey, eat just enough—too much of it, and you will vomit.

Proverbs 25:28
Like a city whose walls are broken down is a man who lacks self-control.

1 Thessalonians 5:6
So then, let us not be like others, who are asleep, but let us be alert and self-controlled.

1 Thessalonians 5:8
But since we belong to the day, let us be self-controlled, putting on faith and love as a breastplate, and the hope of salvation as a helmet.

Titus 2:6
Similarly, encourage the young men to be self-controlled.

1 Peter 5:8–9
Be self-controlled and alert. Your enemy the devil prowls around like a roaring lion looking for someone to devour. Resist him, standing firm in the faith, because you know that your brothers throughout the world are undergoing the same kind of sufferings.

See also: Galatians 5:22–23 🍇 ; 2 Peter 1:5–9 ➕

 **Discussion:**
What are some ways you can lose control of your feelings?[1]

What are some ways you can lose control of your actions?[2]

Does the devil know that you, as a human, have trouble with self-control? Read 1 Peter 5:8–9.

What does 1 Peter 5:8–9 say you can do to help maintain self-control?[3]

Take Action:
Use the questions below to help you decide what area should be your priority in gaining self-control.

◆ Think about the first two discussion questions. Which action or feeling do you have the most trouble controlling?

◆ What are the short-term and long-term consequences of this lack of control?

◆ Does your lack of control in this area affect other people? How?

◆ Would your life be better if you had more control over this area? How?

Now, make an action plan of ways you think will help you gain more self-control in this area. Pray and ask God to help you in this struggle. Find verses that will help you.

Related topics: Habits; Temptation

---

1. Anger, temper tantrums, jealousy; being a crybaby, being too sensitive . . .
2. Giving in to temptations, overeating, oversleeping, saying something you shouldn't, laziness . . .
3. Stay alert, resist the devil, stand firm in the faith.

SELF-RESPECT

 **self-respect - n.** Pride in yourself and your abilities.

Genesis 1:27
So God created man in his own image, in the image of God he created him; male and female he created them.

Psalm 139:13–16
For you created my inmost being; you knit me together in my mother's womb. *I praise you because I am fearfully and wonderfully made;* your works are wonderful, I know that full well. My frame was not hidden from you when I was made in the secret place. When I was woven together in the depths of the earth, your eyes saw my unformed body. All the days ordained for me were written in your book before one of them came to be.

Luke 12:7
"Indeed, the very hairs of your head are all numbered. Don't be afraid; you are worth more than many sparrows."

Acts 10:34–35
Then Peter began to speak: "I now realize how true it is that God does not show favoritism but accepts men from every nation who fear him and do what is right."

1 Corinthians 6:19–20
Do you not know that your body is a temple of the Holy Spirit, who is in you, whom you have received from God? You are not your own; you were bought at a price. Therefore honor God with your body.

See also: Psalm 8:3–5; Isaiah 64:8; Ephesians 2:10

 **Discussion:**
Do you respect yourself? Why or why not?

Did you know that God made you special? Read Psalm 139:13–16, and Luke 12:7.

Docs God play favorites? Read Acts 10:34–35.

Do your actions show that you respect yourself? For example, would you consider or do you do the following:
Younger child: eating too much candy, not resting . . .
Older child: taking drugs, drinking, smoking, engaging in pre-marital sex . . .
Consider these actions in light of 1 Corinthians 6:19–20.

Does your self-respect change when others pick on you or make fun of you? Why should it not? Read all the verses.

Think of the last time you played favorites, made fun of, or picked on somebody. How do you think you affected that person's self-respect?

 **Take Action:**
Self-respect Contract:
Complete the following:

◆ I respect myself because . . .
◆ I respect myself too much to . . .
◆ I do not want to hurt another's self-respect by . . .

Signed: _____

Parenting Tip:
Constantly affirm your child's positive character traits and good qualities. You are the most important factor in helping your child develop self-respect.

SENSITIVITY

> **sensitive - adj. 1.** Easily offended or hurt.
> **2.** Aware of other people's feelings. *The counselor was sensitive to Joelle's problems.*

Psalm 31:24
Be strong and take heart, all you who hope in the LORD.

Proverbs 17:27
A man of knowledge uses words with restraint, and *a man of understanding is even-tempered.*

2 Corinthians 6:3–4, 6
We put no stumbling block in anyone's path, so that our ministry will not be discredited. Rather, as servants of God we commend ourselves in every way: . . . in purity, understanding, patience and kindness; in the Holy Spirit and in sincere love.

Ephesians 4:19
Having lost all sensitivity, they have given themselves over to sensuality so as to indulge in every kind of impurity, with a continual lust for more.

Philippians 4:5
Let your gentleness be evident to all. The Lord is near.

1 Thessalonians 5:14
And we urge you, brothers, warn those who are idle, encourage the timid, help the weak, be patient with everyone.

 **Discussion:**
Are you sensitive to others?

◆ Read 1 Thessalonians 5:14.

◆ Think about each part of the verse. Can you think of a time when you weren't sensitive to someone?

◆ How could you have handled the situation with more sensitivity? Read 2 Corinthians 6:3–4, 6.

Are you too sensitive?

◆ Read the first definition.

◆ What word makes that definition into something unhealthy?

◆ Does this describe you or someone you know?

◆ Read Psalm 31:24 and Proverbs 17:27.

Why do you need to avoid situations that could lead to sin? Read Ephesians 4:19 and see Parenting Tip.

Take Action:
Walk in Others' Shoes:
Practice being sensitive to others by imagining what it would be like to be in their situation. Listen to them and show that you care.

Parenting Tip:
Ephesians 4:19 describes the result of desensitization, which is the continual interaction with something bad so that it no longer seems wrong. Monitor closely what your child sees, hears, and does to make sure that inappropriate input is not desensitizing him.

Related topics: Compassion; Kindness

SHARING

> **share - v. 1.** To divide something between two or more people. **2.** To use together. *My cousins share a house.*

Luke 1:58
Her neighbors and relatives heard that the Lord had shown her great mercy, and they shared her joy.

Luke 3:11
John answered, "The man with two tunics should share with him who has none, and the one who has food should do the same."

Romans 12:13
Share with God's people who are in need. Practice hospitality.

Philippians 4:14
Yet it was good of you to share in my troubles.

1 Timothy 6:18
Command them to do good, to be rich in good deeds, and to *be generous and willing to share.*

Philemon 6
I pray that you may be active in sharing your faith, so that you will have a full understanding of every good thing we have in Christ.

Hebrews 13:16
And do not forget to do good and to share with others, for with such sacrifices God is pleased.

See also: Proverbs 22:9; Isaiah 58:7; Acts 4:32; 2 Corinthians 9:13

Discussion:
What can you share?[1] Read Luke 1:58; 3:11; Philippians 4:14; 1 Timothy 6:18; and Philemon 6.

What is God's response when you share (Hebrews 13:16)?

Take Action:
As you noticed in the first discussion question, each verse deals with a different way of sharing. In which type of sharing do you have a particular interest? Plan a way that you can share in that area.

Parenting Tip:
Younger child: A good way to mediate sharing problems is to teach time-sharing or taking turns. Instruct the children that one of them can play with the toy for a couple of minutes while the other child plays with something else and then switch when the time is up. Help the children keep track of the time. Encourage your child to use this tactic on his own.

Remember to reinforce positive behavior with praise. When you see your child sharing, say things like:

- ◆ "I really like the way you are sharing!"
- ◆ "What a good friend you are to share your favorite toy with (name)!"
- ◆ God is happy that you are sharing!" (Hebrews 13:16)

Older child: The same principles apply to older children as for younger children, but they can be modified according to maturity. For example, set a schedule or time limits for the use of the computer. Remember that older children continue to be encouraged by praise for sharing.

Related topic: Greed

---

1. Your material possessions, faith, joy, sadness, time, energy, hope, love ...

SICKNESS

 **sick - adj.** Suffering from a disease; ill.

Psalm 73:26
My flesh and my heart may fail, but God is the strength of my heart and my portion forever.

Proverbs 18:14
A man's spirit sustains him in sickness, but a crushed spirit who can bear?

Jeremiah 10:19
Woe to me because of my injury! My wound is incurable! Yet I said to myself, "This is my sickness, and I must endure it."

2 Corinthians 4:16
Therefore we do not lose heart. Though outwardly we are wasting away, yet inwardly we are being renewed day by day.

2 Corinthians 12:7–10
To keep me from becoming conceited because of these surpassingly great revelations, there was given me a thorn in my flesh, a messenger of Satan, to torment me. Three times I pleaded with the Lord to take it away from me. But he said to me, "My grace is sufficient for you, for my power is made perfect in weakness." Therefore I will boast all the more gladly about my weaknesses, so that Christ's power may rest on me. That is why, for Christ's sake, I delight in weaknesses, in insults, in hardships, in persecutions, in difficulties. For when I am weak, then I am strong.

See also: Psalm 23:4; Matthew 25:36; John 16:33; Romans 8:23; Philippians 3:20–21; James 5:14–15

Discussion:
According to Proverbs 18:14, what is an important thing to do when you are sick?[1]

Do you or does someone you know have a disability or incurable illness?

- Can you ask God for healing? Read James 5:15.
- Why does God sometimes choose not to heal? Read Jeremiah 10:19 and 2 Corinthians 12:7–10.
- When are you assured to be completely healed if you are a Christian? Look up Philippians 3:20–21.
- Read the encouraging words in Psalm 73:26 and 2 Corinthians 4:16.

 **Take Action:**
Spirit Lifters: Proverbs 18:14
If someone you know is sick:

- Make a-goodie-a-day bag with a different surprise to pull out each day.
- Pray for him. Ask if there are specifics for which you can pray.
- Write a note or make a picture or card to let him know you are praying for him.

If you are sick:
How can you keep your spirits up?

- Read the verses under the topics of Comfort and Hope.
- Immerse yourself in a good book or audio-book tape.
- Play board games.
- Ask for some of your favorite foods.

Related topics: Comfort; Health; Hope; Suffering

1. Keep your spirits up. How? See Take Action.

STEALING

 **steal - v.** To take something that does not belong to you.

Exodus 20:15
"You shall not steal."

Leviticus 19:13
"Do not defraud your neighbor or rob him."

Proverbs 10:2
Ill-gotten treasures are of no value, but righteousness delivers from death.

Ephesians 4:28
He who has been stealing must steal no longer, but must work, doing something useful with his own hands, that he may have something to share with those in need.

Discussion:
What would the world be like if there was no law against stealing?

- Would there be anything left in the stores?
- Would you be able to buy what you need, or would it all be taken unfairly?
- Would you feel safe in your house, or would people commonly break in?

The Bible is clear about stealing. Read the verses listed.

Discuss the old saying, "Finders keepers, losers weepers" (early nineteenth-century proverb).

- Just because you found something, does that make it yours?
- What should you do before keeping something you have found?

Take Action:
Parent: Take a tour of your local prison. Discuss with your child that stealing is a sin and also reaps unpleasant consequences from the law.

Parenting Tip:
What should you do when your child has stolen something?

Always make him take the item back and apologize. For an older child, this may involve reporting him to the police. Do not protect your child from the consequences of his actions. If you do, the child will learn that he can get out of bad situations with your help and will be more likely to do it again.

Having your child return the item and apologize is not a punishment. It is what should be expected. Therefore, also implement an age-appropriate punishment.

STRESS

 **stress - n.** Worry, strain, or pressure. *My dad is under a lot of stress at work.*

Psalm 62:8
Trust in him at all times, O people; pour out your hearts to him, for God is our refuge.

Matthew 11:28–30
"Come to me, all you who are weary and burdened, and I will give you rest. Take my yoke upon you and learn from me, for I am gentle and humble in heart, and you will find rest for your souls. For my yoke is easy and my burden is light."

2 Corinthians 1:8
We do not want you to be uninformed, brothers, about the hardships we suffered in the province of Asia. We were under great pressure, far beyond our ability to endure, so that we despaired even of life.

2 Corinthians 4:8
We are hard pressed on every side, but not crushed; perplexed, but not in despair.

2 Corinthians 11:28
Besides everything else, I face daily the pressure of my concern for all the churches.

1 Peter 5:7
Cast all your anxiety on him because he cares for you.

See also: Isaiah 40:27–31; John 14:1; 1 Corinthians 1:3–4; James 5:10–11

 **Discussion:**
Discuss situations that have put you under stress.

◆ How do you react to stress?[1]

◆ Does God care about your stress? Read 1 Peter 5:7.

What are some positive ways of dealing with stress?

◆ Pour it out to God. Read Psalm 62:8.

◆ Talk to someone else who can help you put things in perspective.

◆ Think about "What's the worst thing that could happen if . . . (fill in the scenario)?" Would you be able to handle that happening? Now look at your stress again. Is it worth it?

Take Action:
1. Are you stressed? Read all of the Bible verses listed. Work through the ways of dealing with stress listed in the Discussion section.

2. Do you know someone who is stressed? Ask if you can help by:

◆ Listening

◆ Assisting in some way

◆ Praying

Parenting Tip:
Your child may be under more stress than you realize. Remember that situations are relative to past experiences. Just because you do not see something as a big deal does not mean it is not for the child.

Related topic: Worry

---

1. Moodiness and physical symptoms, among others.

SUFFERING

> **suffer - v. I.** To have pain, discomfort, or sorrow. **2.** To experience or undergo something unpleasant.

Nahum 1:7
The LORD is good, a refuge in times of trouble. He cares for those who trust in him.

John 16:33
"I have told you these things, so that in me you may have peace. In this world you will have trouble. But take heart! I have overcome the world."

Romans 5:2b–5
And we rejoice in the hope of the glory of God. Not only so, but we also rejoice in our sufferings, because we know that suffering produces perseverance; perseverance, character; and character, hope. And hope does not disappoint us, because God has poured out his love into our hearts by the Holy Spirit, whom he has given us.

Romans 8:18
I consider that our present sufferings are not worth comparing with the glory that will be revealed in us.

1 Corinthians 12:26
[In reference to the body of Christ, the church] If one part suffers, every part suffers with it; if one part is honored, every part rejoices with it.

See also: Psalms 55:22; 119:50; Romans 8:38–39; 2 Corinthians 1:3–7; 4:16–18; 1 Peter 2:20–21; 4:12–13; 5:7–11

 **Discussion:**

Ask your grandparents or senior citizen friends if they or anybody they know have made it through life without suffering.

Find time to discuss with your grandparents and godly older people some of the trials, heartaches, and suffering they have encountered throughout their lifetime. Ask them for advice on how to cope with suffering.

How can you look at suffering in a positive light? Read Romans 5:2b–5.

What does 1 Corinthians 12:26 have to say about suffering?

- Can you think of specific examples from within your church?

Read and discuss Nahum 1:7; John 16:33; and Romans 8:18 and share how each is a comfort.

Take Action:

1. Discuss and memorize the following saying:

- "This, too, shall pass."

    —Nineteenth-century proverb

2. Do you know someone who is suffering? How can you help him or her? Be creative.

3. Are you suffering? Let God help you through this time. Call on fellow believers for support and encouragement. Read Nahum 1:7 and 1 Corinthians 12:26.

Related topic: Perseverance

SYMPATHY

 **sympathy - n.** The understanding and sharing of other people's troubles. *After her accident, Yoko's friends gave her lots of sympathy.*

Psalm 69:20
Scorn has broken my heart and has left me helpless; I looked for sympathy, but there was none, for comforters, but I found none.

Romans 12:15
Rejoice with those who rejoice; mourn with those who mourn.

Ephesians 4:32a
Be kind and compassionate to one another.

1 Peter 3:8
Finally, all of you, live in harmony with one another; *be sympathetic,* love as brothers, be compassionate and humble.

 **Discussion:**
Think of a recent situation when you were sad.

◆ Was there anyone who shared these sorrows with you?

◆ How did it help you?

◆ How did the sympathy make you feel?

Read Romans 12:15 and 1 Peter 3:8 and brainstorm ways to show sympathy in the following situations:

❖ Your friend tells you that his grandmother passed away.

  ◆ Be a shoulder to cry on.

  ◆ Send a card and/or flowers.

  ◆ Take food to the family.

❖ Your little sister failed her math test.

  ◆ Offer to tutor her with her math homework and help her study for the next test.

  ◆ Encourage her—be her cheerleader!

❖ Your father lost his job.

  ◆ Make a card telling him you love him and that the only job that matters to you is his job of being Dad.

  ◆ Make an effort not to whine or ask for material wants during the time he is out of a job.

  ◆ Tell him you will pray that God will lead him in the right direction and provide the perfect new job.

❖ Your mother has the flu.

  ◆ Clip flowers from the yard and bring them to her room to make it more cheerful.

  ◆ Be a helper: Bring her a bell that she can ring when she wants or needs anything.

Take Action:
Put Romans 12:15 into practice. Think of someone who is rejoicing or mourning. Call him, write a note, or visit him and show sympathy or rejoice with him.

TALENT

talent - n. A natural ability or skill.
gift - n. A special talent.

I Corinthians 12:12

The body is a unit, though it is made of up many parts; and though all its parts are many, they form one body. So it is with Christ.

I Corinthians 12:27

Now you are the body of Christ, and each one of you is a part of it.

Ephesians 4:16

From him the whole body, joined and held together by every supporting ligament, grows and builds itself up in love, as each part does its work.

Colossians 3:17

And whatever you do, whether in word or deed, do it all in the name of the Lord Jesus, giving thanks to God the Father through him.

I Peter 4:10–11

Each one should use whatever gift he has received to serve others, faithfully administering God's grace in its various forms. If anyone speaks, he should do it as one speaking the very words of God. If anyone serves, he should do it with the strength God provides, so that in all things God may be praised through Jesus Christ. To him be the glory and the power for ever and ever. Amen.

See also: Romans 12:6–8; 2 Corinthians 9:1–2

 **Discussion:**
In what areas do you think you are talented and gifted? Make a list.

The Bible uses the human body and its parts as an analogy for individuals and the special talents and gifts they bring to the body of Christ, the church. Read 1 Corinthians 12:12.

- ◆ Think about and discuss all the people who use their talents and gifts to make your church's activities and ministries run smoothly.

- ◆ Did you know that God made you special by giving you particular gifts? Read Ephesians 4:16 and 1 Corinthians 12:27.

- ◆ Look up and read 1 Corinthians 12:14–27 to find out how you and "the body" are designed to work together.

How can you use your talents and gifts to serve God? Read Colossians 3:17 and 1 Peter 4:10–11.

Take Action:
How can you use your talents and gifts? Ideas:

- ◆ If you are artistic, draw pictures, and mail or deliver them to the homebound members of your church.

- ◆ If you have the gift of hospitality, help make newcomers feel welcome in Sunday school, public school, and other activities in which you are involved.

- ◆ If you enjoy teaching, read or tell Bible stories to a younger brother or sister or to friends when they come over.

Now think of your own ideas that relate to your specific talents, abilities, or gifts; and take action.

Related topic: Ministry

TEMPTATION

> **tempt - v. I.** If you **tempt** someone, you try to get the person to do or want something that is wrong or foolish.

Psalm 19:13
Keep your servant also from willful sins; may they not rule over me. Then will I be blameless, innocent of great transgression.

I Corinthians 10:12–13
So, if you think you are standing firm, be careful that you don't fall! No temptation has seized you except what is common to man. And God is faithful; *he will not let you be tempted beyond what you can bear.* But when you are tempted, he will also provide a way out so that you can stand up under it.

Ephesians 6:10–11 🛡
Finally, be strong in the Lord and in his mighty power. Put on the full armor of God so that you can take your stand against the devil's schemes.

Hebrews 4:15
For we do not have a high priest who is unable to sympathize with our weaknesses, but we have one who has been tempted in every way, just as we are—yet was without sin.

I Peter 5:8–9a
Be self-controlled and alert. Your enemy the devil prowls around like a roaring lion looking for someone to devour. Resist him, standing firm in the faith.

See also: Proverbs 1:10; Matthew 6:13; Romans 6:14, 19; 2 Corinthians 10:4; 1 Thessalonians 5:22; 2 Thessalonians 3:3; 2 Timothy 2:22; James 1:13–15; 4:7–8a

Discussion:
Do you think the devil knows your weaknesses?
Read 1 Peter 5:8–9.

How do you go about resisting the devil?[1] Read Ephesians
6:10–11 and see 1 Peter 5:8–9a.

Read 1 Corinthians 10:12–13.

- ◆ Do you sometimes think that you will never be tempted by a particular sin? Pay attention to the first sentence of this passage.
- ◆ Is there any temptation that you can't resist? Pay attention to the third sentence of this passage.
- ◆ How does God help you so you can resist? Pay attention to the last two sentences of this passage.

Can Jesus understand what you are going through? See Hebrews 4:15.

Take Action:
Pray against temptation. When saying your daily
prayers, ask for strength and protection in the areas
with which you are struggling. Pray also that you will be on
your guard in the areas in which you are standing firm. Pray
Psalm 19:13 and look up Matthew 6:13.

Parenting Tip:
As you hear news reports and stories of things that
happen to other children, make a point to ask your child,
"What would you have done in that situation?" Or, "What
would you do if _____ happened?" These questions will
make him think and help equip him to battle temptation more
adequately because of his preparedness.

---

1. "Standing firm in the faith."

THANKFULNESS

 **thank - v.** To tell someone that you are grateful. *We thanked him for the ride.*

Psalm 100:4–5

Enter his gates with thanksgiving and his courts with praise; *give thanks to him and praise his name.* For the LORD is good and his love endures forever; his faithfulness continues through all generations.

2 Corinthians 9:15

Thanks be to God for his indescribable gift!

Ephesians 5:19b–20

Sing and make music in your heart to the Lord, always giving thanks to God the Father for everything, in the name of our Lord Jesus Christ.

Colossians 4:2

Devote yourselves to prayer, being watchful and thankful.

1 Thessalonians 1:2

We always thank God for all of you, mentioning you in our prayers.

1 Thessalonians 5:16–18

Be joyful always; pray continually; *give thanks in all circumstances, for this is God's will for you in Christ Jesus.*

Hebrews 12:28–29

Therefore, since we are receiving a kingdom that cannot be shaken, let us be thankful, and so worship God acceptably with reverence and awe, for our "God is a consuming fire."

See also: Psalm 100; Philippians 1:3; Colossians 2:6–7

 **Discussion:**
For what are you thankful?

How often do you thank God for these things?

Do you daily thank God for who He is and what He has done? Read and discuss the verses.

Is there a situation in which you could not find something about which to be thankful? Read 1 Thessalonians 5:16–18.

Think of the worst possible situation that could happen. Discuss ways to be thankful even in the midst of those circumstances.

 **Take Action:**
1. *Parent:* Help your child learn appreciation by having him always write thank you notes. An extension is to encourage thank-you notes for acts of kindness.

2. *Thankfulness Book (Family Project):*

> ➤ Give each member of the family a piece of paper.
> ➤ Instruct each person to compile a list of all the things for which he or she is thankful.
> ➤ Work on the list for several days individually.
> ➤ Then come together and share with each other and God what you are thankful for.
> ➤ Bind the pages into a book format and save it as a family keepsake.
> ➤ *Younger children:* Look through magazines and cut out pictures to make a thankfulness collage.

3. Memorize Psalm 100. Since it is a psalm, try making up a tune for it, or put it to a familiar tune.

Related topics: Appreciation; Cheerfulness; Joyfulness

TOLERANCE

 **tolerance - n. 1.** The willingness to respect or accept the customs, beliefs, or opinions of others.

Micah 4:4–5
Every man will sit under his own vine and under his own fig tree, and no one will make them afraid, for the LORD Almighty has spoken. All the nations may walk in the name of their gods; we will walk in the name of the LORD our God for ever and ever.

Romans 14:5–6a
One man considers one day more sacred than another; another man considers every day alike. Each one should be fully convinced in his own mind. He who regards one day as special, does so to the Lord.

Ephesians 4:2
Be completely humble and gentle; be patient, bearing with one another in love.

1 Peter 3:15
But in your hearts set apart Christ as Lord. Always be prepared to give an answer to everyone who asks you to give the reason for the hope that you have. But do this with gentleness and respect.

Discussion:

Does tolerance mean you have to agree with another's viewpoint?[1] Read the definition.

Discuss a recent time when you had to tolerate someone else's viewpoint. Read Micah 4:4–5 and Romans 14:5–6a.

Is there ever a time when you should be intolerant?

* Imagine that a friend wants you to lie about how a vase was broken while the two of you were rough-housing. You tell your friend you don't want to lie because the Bible says it's wrong. Your friend says he doesn't believe in the Bible and doesn't think it's wrong to lie in this case since it won't make the vase any less broken. Should you tolerate your friend's belief in this case?

* Answer: No, you should never compromise your values or standards. The line for tolerance must be drawn when it comes to your having to make a choice between right and wrong.

How should you react when someone is intolerant of your beliefs? Read Ephesians 4:2 and 1 Peter 3:15.

Take Action:

Look and listen for examples of tolerance or intolerance in your daily life or on the news. Ask yourself the following questions and discuss them with the family.

* What does God's Word say about this?

* Should we be tolerant of this? Or should we stand firm and obey God's Word?

---

1. No, you can respect someone's viewpoint without agreeing, just as you hope others will respect your beliefs.

TRUST

 **trust - v.** If you **trust** someone, you believe that he or she is honest and reliable.

Psalm 20:7
Some trust in chariots and some in horses, but we trust in the name of the LORD our God.

Psalm 37:3–6
Trust in the LORD and do good; dwell in the land and enjoy safe pasture. Delight yourself in the LORD and he will give you the desires of your heart. Commit your way to the LORD; trust in him and he will do this: He will make your righteousness shine like the dawn, the justice of your cause like the noonday sun.

Psalm 49:13–15
This is the fate of those who trust in themselves, and of their followers, who approve their sayings. Like sheep they are destined for the grave, and death will feed on them. The upright will rule over them in the morning; their forms will decay in the grave, far from their princely mansions. But God will redeem my life from the grave; he will surely take me to himself.

Proverbs 3:5–6
Trust in the LORD with all your heart and lean not on your own understanding; in all your ways acknowledge him, and he will make your paths straight.

Luke 16:10
"Whoever can be trusted with very little can also be trusted with much, and whoever is dishonest with very little will also be dishonest with much."

See also: Genesis 39:2–4

Discussion:
Read Luke 16:10.

◆ Discuss real-life examples of this principle.

◆ What are the benefits of being trustworthy?

◆ How do you know whether or not other people are trustworthy?

◆ Are you trustworthy?

Look up and read Genesis 39:2–4 to learn how Joseph was entrusted with much because he trusted the Lord and had proved himself trustworthy.

In what do some people trust for their "salvation"?[1] Read Psalm 20:7.

What happens if you try to trust in yourself rather than God? Read Psalm 49:13–15.

What does the Lord promise to do if you trust in Him? Read Psalm 37:3–6 and Proverbs 3:5–6.

Take Action:
Parent: Give your child a chance to build her trustworthiness by putting Luke 16:10 into practice. For example: Agree to get a pet if the child shows that she diligently takes care of a fish for a set period of time.

Parenting Tip:
Your child must be able to trust your word. Avoid saying things like "Next week we will go to the movie," if you have no intention of following through. Similarly, avoid saying, "Next time you do that you will get in trouble," unless you are truly going to follow up. Everything you say will either breed trust or distrust, so make sure you think before speaking.

---

1. Success, money, popularity, people, idols, good works ...

WEARINESS

 **weary - adj. 1.** Very tired, or exhausted. *We were weary after the long trip.* **2.** Having little patience or interest; bored. *James grew weary of eating the same lunch every day.*

Isaiah 40:28–31

Do you not know? Have you not heard? The LORD is the everlasting God, the Creator of the ends of the earth. He will not grow tired or weary, and his understanding no one can fathom. He gives strength to the weary and increases the power of the weak. Even youths grow tired and weary, and young men stumble and fall; but those who hope in the LORD will renew their strength. They will soar on wings like eagles; they will run and not grow weary, they will walk and not be faint.

Matthew 11:28

"Come to me, all you who are weary and burdened, and I will give you rest."

Galatians 6:9

Let us not become weary in doing good, for at the proper time we will reap a harvest if we do not give up.

Hebrews 12:3

Consider him who endured such opposition from sinful men, so that you will not grow weary and lose heart.

 Discussion:

Have you ever been so physically, emotionally, or mentally exhausted that you thought you could not go on?

How can God help you when you are weary? Read Isaiah 40:28–31; Matthew 11:28; and Hebrews 12:3.

Read Galatians 6:9. Do you ever get weary of doing good? Think of some examples of reaping a harvest for not giving up in doing good.

Take Action:

Are you weary today or do you know someone who is weary?

◆ Draw a picture of the last sentence of Isaiah 40:28–31 to remind you or someone else of that verse.

◆ Pray that verse for you or the other person. Ask God for the strength to make it through this time of weariness.

Parenting Tips:

1. It is your responsibility to make sure your child gets the rest he needs. At night, if the child says that he is not sleepy, insist that he lie down and get some rest. Teach thankfulness for the time God gives us to rest and sleep to help make our bodies strong.

2. Be careful not to overinvolve your child in extracurricular activities. Each year, give him a choice of several activities and let him pick, with your guidance, however many activities you think are appropriate.

WORRY

 **worry - n.** To be anxious or uneasy about something.

Proverbs 12:25
An anxious heart weighs a man down, but a kind word cheers him up.

Matthew 6:25–27
"Therefore I tell you, do not worry about your life, what you will eat or drink; or about your body, what you will wear. Is not life more important than food, and the body more important than clothes? Look at the birds of the air; they do not sow or reap or store away in barns, and yet your heavenly Father feeds them. Are you not much more valuable than they? *Who of you by worrying can add a single hour to his life?*"

Matthew 6:34
"Therefore do not worry about tomorrow, for tomorrow will worry about itself. Each day has enough trouble of its own."

Philippians 4:6–7
Do not be anxious about anything, but in everything, by prayer and petition, with thanksgiving, present your requests to God. And the peace of God, which transcends all understanding, will guard your hearts and your minds in Christ Jesus.

1 Peter 5:7
Cast all your anxiety on him because he cares for you.

See also: Psalms 55:22; 94:19; 139:23; Matthew 6:28–33

 **Discussion:**
Do you worry?

+ Does it ever help the situation?
+ Discuss Matthew 6:25–27 and Matthew 6:34.

Read Philippians 4:6–7.

+ Is any worry too small to give to God?
+ How does the passage indicate we should present our requests to God?
+ What does the passage say happens when we give our anxieties to God?

How can you help others when they are worried? Read Proverbs 12:25.

 **Take Action:**
Do I Peter 5:7:

Younger child: Decorate a paper bag or jar and label it "Worry Jar." Pick one of the verses and write it on the container. Then help your child write out his worries on slips of paper. Pray over the slips as you put them in the container. Encourage the child to try not to be anxious about these things because he has given them to God. Open the bag sometime later and discuss how God helped him through the worries and whether or not it was worth the anxiety.

Older child/youth: Encourage your child to keep a prayer journal. When he is feeling anxious or stressed about something, he can pour it out to God in his journal and leave it with Him. Later on, he can read back through his journal and see how God has answered his prayers. It will serve as a good record of past trials and an encouragement of how God ultimately works things out for the best.

SCRIPTURE APPENDIX

The following symbols are given as an aid to help you recognize that a particular Scripture text is pulled from a longer passage. When you see the pictures on the Scripture pages throughout the book, refer to the following pages for the complete passage.

KEY TO COMPLETE SCRIPTURE PASSAGES

The Ten Commandments

The Beatitudes

The Love Chapter

The Fruit of the Spirit

The Armor of God

Clothe Yourself with . . .

Add to Your Faith . . .

THE TEN COMMANDMENTS
Exodus 20:1–17
And God spoke all these words:

"I am the LORD your God, who brought you out of Egypt, out of the land of slavery.

"You shall have no other gods before me.

"You shall not make for yourself an idol in the form of anything in heaven above or on the earth beneath or in the waters below. You shall not bow down to them or worship them; for I, the LORD your God, am a jealous God, punishing the children for the sin of the fathers to the third and fourth generation of those who hate me, but showing love to a thousand generations of those who love me and keep my commandments.

"You shall not misuse the name of the LORD your God, for the LORD will not hold anyone guiltless who misuses his name.

"Remember the Sabbath day by keeping it holy. Six days you shall labor and do all your work, but the seventh day is a Sabbath to the LORD your God. On it you shall not do any work, neither you, nor your son or daughter, nor your manservant or maidservant, nor your animals, nor the alien within your gates. For in six days the LORD made the heavens and the earth, the sea, and all that is in them, but he rested on the seventh day. Therefore the LORD blessed the Sabbath day and made it holy.

"Honor your father and your mother, so that you may live long in the land the LORD your God is giving you.

"You shall not murder.

"You shall not commit adultery.

"You shall not steal.

"You shall not give false testimony against your neighbor.

"You shall not covet your neighbor's house. You shall not covet your neighbor's wife, or his manservant or maidservant, his ox or donkey, or anything that belongs to your neighbor."

☺   ☺   ☺   ☺   ☺   ☺   ☺

THE BEATITUDES
Matthew 5:3–12
"Blessed are the poor in spirit,
    for theirs is the kingdom of heaven.
Blessed are those who mourn,
    for they will be comforted.
Blessed are the meek,
    for they will inherit the earth.
Blessed are those who hunger and thirst
    for righteousness,
    for they will be filled.
Blessed are the merciful,
    for they will be shown mercy.
Blessed are the pure in heart,
    for they will see God.
Blessed are the peacemakers,
    for they will be called sons of God.
Blessed are those who are persecuted
    because of righteousness,
    for theirs is the kingdom of heaven.

"Blessed are you when people insult you, persecute you and falsely say all kinds of evil against you because of me. Rejoice and be glad, because great is your reward in heaven, for in the same way they persecuted the prophets who were before you."

THE LOVE CHAPTER
1 Corinthians 13

If I speak in the tongues of men and of angels, but have not love, I am only a resounding gong or a clanging cymbal. If I have the gift of prophecy and can fathom all mysteries and all knowledge, and if I have a faith that can move mountains, but have not love, I am nothing. If I give all I possess to the poor and surrender my body to the flames, but have not love, I gain nothing.

Love is patient, love is kind. It does not envy, it does not boast, it is not proud. It is not rude, it is not self-seeking, it is not easily angered, it keeps no record of wrongs. Love does not delight in evil but rejoices with the truth. It always protects, always trusts, always hopes, always perseveres.

Love never fails. But where there are prophecies, they will cease; where there are tongues, they will be stilled; where there is knowledge, it will pass away. For we know in part and we prophesy in part, but when perfections comes, the imperfect disappears. When I was a child, I talked like a child, I thought like a child, I reasoned like a child. When I became a man, I put childish ways behind me. Now we see but a poor reflection as in a mirror; then we shall see face to face. Now I know in part; then I shall know fully, even as I am fully known.

And now these three remain: faith, hope and love. But the greatest of these is love.

THE FRUIT OF THE SPIRIT
Galatians 5:22–25
But the fruit of the Spirit is love, joy, peace, patience, kindness, goodness, faithfulness, gentleness and self-control. Against such things there is no law. Those who belong to Christ Jesus have crucified the sinful nature with its passions and desires. Since we live by the Spirit, let us keep in step with the Spirit.

THE ARMOR OF GOD
Ephesians 6:10–18
Finally, be strong in the Lord and in his mighty power. Put on the full armor of God so that you can take your stand against the devil's schemes. For our struggle is not against flesh and blood, but against the rulers, against the authorities, against the powers of this dark world and against the spiritual forces of evil in the heavenly realms. Therefore put on the full armor of God, so that when the day of evil comes, you may be able to stand your ground, and after you have done everything, to stand. Stand firm then, with the belt of truth buckled around your waist, with the breastplate of righteousness in place, and with your feet fitted with the readiness that comes from the gospel of peace. In addition to all this, take up the shield of faith, with which you can extinguish all the flaming arrows of the evil one. Take the helmet of salvation and the sword of the Spirit, which is the word of God. And pray in the Spirit on all occasions with all kinds of prayers and requests. With this in mind, be alert and always keep on praying for all the saints.

CLOTHE YOURSELVES WITH ...
Colossians 3:12–14
Therefore, as God's chosen people, holy and dearly loved, clothe yourselves with compassion, kindness, humility, gentleness and patience. Bear with each other and forgive whatever grievances you may have against one another. Forgive as the Lord forgave you. And over all these virtues put on love, which binds them all together in perfect unity.

ADD TO YOUR FAITH ...
2 Peter 1:5–9
For this very reason, make every effort to add to your faith goodness; and to goodness, knowledge; and to knowledge, self-control; and to self-control, perseverance; and to perseverance, godliness; and to godliness, brotherly kindness; and to brotherly kindness, love. For if you possess these qualities in increasing measure, they will keep you from being ineffective and unproductive in your knowledge of our Lord Jesus Christ. But if anyone does not have them, he is nearsighted and blind, and has forgotten that he has been cleansed from his past sins.

CROSS-REFERENCE INDEX